THE DOCTRINE OF THE TRINITY

THE DOCTRINE OF THE TRINITY

BY

R. S. FRANKS

M.A., D.LITT., LL.D.

PRINCIPAL EMERITUS OF THE
WESTERN COLLEGE, BRISTOL

GERALD DUCKWORTH AND CO. LTD.
3 *Henrietta Street, London, W.C.*2

First published 1953
All rights reserved

Made and Printed in Great Britain by
The Camelot Press Ltd., London and Southampton

TABLE OF CONTENTS

Part I

THE NEW TESTAMENT MATRIX

Part II

THE PATRISTIC DEVELOPMENT

Part III

ASSIMILATION, CRITICISM AND RECONSTRUCTION

THE DOCTRINE OF THE TRINITY

I.—THE NEW TESTAMENT MATRIX

1. INTRODUCTION

TO write on the doctrine of the Trinity is to undertake a difficult and venturesome task. There come to mind the words of Thomas à Kempis in *The Imitation of Christ* (I, 1, 3): 'What will it avail thee to argue profoundly of the Trinity, if thou be void of humility, and are thereby displeasing to the Trinity?'

But it is not always true humility to avoid argument. It is impossible for a Christian theologian to ignore the sharp controversy over the doctrine of the Trinity. How differently men have thought about it! Newman in his *Grammar of Assent*, taking the Athanasian Creed as the authoritative expression of the doctrine, calls it 'the most simple and sublime, the most devotional formulary to which Christianity has given birth'. For Matthew Arnold in *Literature and Dogma* the same creed was 'the fairy-tale of the three Lord Shaftesburys'. Between the exultation of the one and the mockery of the other there are many intermediate positions. It is best to recognize that the doctrine of the Trinity has been matter of debate throughout the Christian centuries and still is so. It is therefore necessary that the issue should be discussed with the best means at our disposal. It is not satisfactory to take refuge in the common notion that it is a mystery. It is the result of a rational and intelligible process, and its value can only be appreciated through a study of this process.

Such a study this book is to undertake. Its moderate scale will compel a limitation to essentials, which may not be altogether a disadvantage, since it may prevent our losing 'the wood' in 'the trees'. The formation of the doctrine of the Trinity will appear as an argument from history to a metaphysic as the solid basis that gives meaning to the history. It sprang from the reaction upon Jewish monotheism of belief in the Divine mission of Jesus Christ and the experience of the power of the Holy Spirit in the Christian Church. It issued in a doctrine of One God in Three Persons, understood as an intimate knowledge of the Divine Being. The ultimate aim of the doctrine was to show how God could be both One and Three.

Since Jewish monotheism itself is traced by Christians to Divine revelation, there are three fundamental acts of God in history, the recognition of which forms the basis of the doctrine of the Trinity. There is first of all God's choice of Israel as His peculiar people. To them He became known under the sacred name of JAHWEH, and with them he made a covenant which is expressed in the words, 'I will be their God and they shall be my people' (Jer. xxxi. 33). Second comes the sending of Jesus, who was born of the stock of Israel; and third is the gift of the Holy Spirit to the Church, which is the Society of those confessing Jesus as Messiah or Christ. God chose, God sent, God gave: the acknowledgment of these three great moments of Divine revelation is our starting point.

It is important to observe here that it is the second or central act which was the original disturbing factor that set in motion the transformation of Jewish monotheism into the Christian doctrine of the Trinity. It was the sending of Jesus Christ into the world which both reacted upon the doctrine of God and produced a revision of Old Testament conceptions of the Spirit. The doctrines of the Trinity and the Incarnation are therefore so interwoven that it is impossible to study the doctrine of the Trinity without at least keeping an eye on the doctrine of the Incarnation. Nowhere is this regard to the doctrine of the Incarnation more necessary than in dealing with the New Testament, where there is a much further advance towards a doctrine of the Incarnation than towards that of the Trinity. It is important to observe this now, because if we are to proceed historically, it is with the New Testament that we must begin. It is here that we first see the troubling of the waters of Jewish monotheism by the advent of Jesus Christ.

At this stage we do not consider the New Testament as the authoritative source of Christian doctrine, which it afterwards became, together with the Old Testament. We shall come to that way of regarding it, as we go on. Now we consider the books of the New Testament in their original inception and character. When they were written, the only authority recognized by the Christian Church was the Old Testament, the sacred book of the Jewish people, whose central theme is God's choice of Israel. The New Testament writings at first lacked a similar authoritative status; they were, however, important to the Church as charismatic works written for its edification. *Charismata*, or gifts of grace, were universal in the primitive Church (I Cor. xii. 7), and the gift of writing for edification was one of them (Rev. i. 10, 11). There were many other charismatic works in the first age of the Church besides those preserved in the New Testament. The New Testament books were selected from the whole number of such works in the second and third centuries: they were then made authoritative along with the Old Testament on the assumption of their apostolic origin and doctrine. There is no doubt that in the main the Church was guided by a sound instinct: the most important books in the New Testament do truly represent the Apostolic Christianity of the first century, though some marginal works that were included in it differ little from some other marginal works that were excluded.

It is then as charismatic writings representing Apostolic Christianity that we have to deal with the books of the New Testament. They show us the Church, standing on the Old Testament, but endeavouring to assimilate the great new facts of Christ and the Spirit in its midst. In the process the Old Testament itself furnishes many of the conceptions utilized; but other ideas are brought in, both from the later Jewish theology, and from Hellenistic thought. Looked at in this way, the New Testament represents the matrix in which the doctrine of the Trinity is beginning to be formed.

This would seem to be the place to protest strongly against the idea that there is no substantial Hellenism in the New Testament, though it was written in Greek for Greek-speaking and therefore Greek-thinking people. The idea has often been asserted, but has never found more brilliant expression than in Cullmann's recent book *Christ and Time* (*Christus und die Zeit*, 1946, E.T., 1951). It is, however, demonstrably false, as will presently be shown. There has been too much in theology of the maxim, 'timeo Danaos, et dona ferentes'. I Cor. i. 23, 'Christ crucified, to Jews a scandal and to Greeks folly', has been exploited to the complete forgetfulness that Paul also wrote in the same epistle, 'I am become all things to all men, that I may save some' (ix. 22). All the three factors above mentioned have contributed to New Testament Christology and therefore to the inception of the doctrine of the Trinity.

It has been said that the New Testament represents the matrix in which the doctrine of the Trinity begins to he formed. Passages of a directly Trinitarian complexion are, however, few in number, and in no case amount to the definite statement of a doctrine. What we actually find is just the putting together in a suggestive way of the names of the Father, the Son and the Holy Spirit, notably in the benediction of II Cor. xiii. 14 and the baptismal formula of Mt. xxviii. 19. Longer passages of the same kind are I Cor. xii. 4–6, Eph. iv. 4–6, I Pet. i. 1–2 and Jude 20, 21. The verse I Jn. v. 7 in the Authorized Version has no support in the best manuscripts, and has disappeared from the Revised Version without leaving even so much as a trace in the margin.

The real evidence for the doctrine of the Trinity to be found in the New Testament is not in such texts as the above, but must be collected by a wider survey, which is above all directed to the developing Christology, but also looks to what is said of God and the Spirit in connection with it. There must be also some consideration of the history which compelled the production of new doctrine. For though the New Testament narratives were written not for historical study but for the support of faith, yet the advent of Christ in history is the foundation of all Christology, and apart from it a doctrine of the Trinity would be mere speculation.

2. PALESTINIAN CHRISTIANITY

Looking at the New Testament in the way we have been describing, there is no doubt where to begin. The germ of the whole doctrinal development is in the original *kerygma* or Apostolic preaching, an account of which we have in the early chapters of Acts, and also in a short form in I Cor. xv. 1–11. Paul lays stress on the fact that the *kerygma* was common to him and the original apostles (xv. 11). His account of the *kerygma* is much the earlier of the two records. Nevertheless, the witness of Acts is to be preferred for our starting-point. It is contained in a succession of Peter's speeches: Acts ii. 14–36, 38, 39, iii. 12–26, iv. 8–12, v. 29–32, x. 34–43. It is clear that behind the record in Acts there are original sources of information, which constitute a reliable witness to the belief of the period before Paul came on the scene. It is highly probable that the sources were written in Aramaic. Thus Acts, though written towards the end of the first century and so considerably later than I Cor. carries us back to an earlier form of the *kerygma*. Its originality is strikingly marked by an important point of difference from the Pauline account. Peter's speeches do not contain the teaching, so central for Paul, that 'Christ died for our sins according to the Scriptures' (I Cor. xv. 3). The forgiveness of sins is regarded by Peter simply as a Messianic gift, like that of the Holy Spirit (Acts ii. 38, v. 31), while the death of Jesus is viewed as a Jewish crime to be repented of (Acts ii. 23, iii. 14). No doubt the reference to prophecy to explain the suffering of Christ (iii. 18), especially the reference to Isa. 53 which is implied by the title 'Servant' given to Him (Acts ii. 13–26, iv. 27–30), contained the presage of a doctrine of Christ's death for our sins according to the Scriptures, such as we find in the Pauline version of the *kerygma*. But the fact remains that Peter is satisfied to speak of forgiveness as Christ's royal gift without introducing any doctrine of Christ's sacrifice anywhere: this is a definite reason for preferring Acts as our starting-point. But there is another reason also. It is that Paul's summary of the *kerygma* in I Cor. xv is inadequate unless it is supplemented by inferences from other parts of his epistles: these inferences can only be made by means of a reference to the fuller *kerygma* of Acts. The account of Acts is therefore the place where we must begin.

To understand the Petrine *kerygma* we have to remember that those addressed in the first four speeches were Jews; the fifth speech was spoken to Gentiles. We shall consider the two cases separately.

Peter in addressing Jews naturally starts from beliefs common to them and himself, a Jewish Christian. We may name three in particular, Jewish monotheism, the Messianic expectation, and the connection with it of the gift of the Spirit. All three need some explanation, if we are to understand the implications of the Petrine *kerygma*.

A fervent belief in One Only God, exalted in righteousness was the absolute foundation of Jewish religion. Jewish monotheism was a living faith in a living God, the Creator of the world, but especially the covenant God of His people Israel. If in the early days of Israelite history the existence of other gods had been recognized, though not their worship, those days were long past. In New Testament times Jewish monotheism had long been firmly established, and was regarded by the Jews themselves as their special distinction among the nations. In their sacred book, the Old Testament, they had a history of God's covenant with them and a standing monument of monotheistic faith. The first article in the creed of Judaism was taken from Deut. vi. 4, which proclaims the Unity of God. It should be mentioned here that though the One God was known to Israel originally by the name of JAHWEH, there was substituted for it in reading the Old Testament *Adonai*, a peculiar form of *Adoni*, 'My Lord', the name JAHWEH being regarded as too sacred for utterance. The Greek translators of the Old Testament accordingly replaced JAHWEH with Κύριος, Lord. It is this usage that we find in Old Testament quotations in the New Testament. The point will come up in interpreting Peter's speeches.

The next matter to be considered is Messianic prophecy. If the law is the first content of the Old Testament and the rule of Jewish life, next to the law came the prophets; and in the days when Peter spoke, Jewish faith struggling against the problem imposed upon it by subjection to Rome, commonly encouraged itself with the expectation of the displacement of the empire of Rome by the Kingdom of God and the advent of His Messiah, or viceregent in

His Kingdom. Those things the prophets had foretold; moreover, since the Canon of prophecy had been closed, their work of prediction had been continued in the numerous pseudonymous Apocalypses which further kindled and fed Jewish hopes. It is true that in some forms of the expectation of the Kingdom of God the Messiah does not appear; but it is the Messianic form of it which forms the background of the Petrine *kerygma,* and of New Testament faith in general. The fundamental Old Testament passages for the conception of the Messiah are Isa. ix. 6–7 and xi. 1–9. Common to both is the prophecy that the Messiah will be a Davidic king, but also that he will transcend common humanity. Out of these two elements in later times grew two different forms of the Messianic expectation, one that of a national monarch ruling in Jerusalem as in the 'Psalms of Solomon' xvii (Pharisaic psalms of the first century B.C.), the other that of an altogether heavenly and transcendent Being, ruling not just over Israel in Palestine, but over a renewed heaven and earth. The great example of the latter conception is found in the 'Similitudes' of the Ethiopic Apocalypse of Enoch (I Enoch), xxxvii–lxxi (chapters which belong also to the first century B.C.). Here the Messiah is pre-existent, before the creation, a Being like an angel dwelling with God in heaven. He is called the Elect and the Son of Man, and is to be the Judge of angels and men. In his name there is salvation.

As to the names by which God's viceregent in His Kingdom was called, (1) the name 'Messiah' (Heb. *mashiach*), meaning 'Anointed', though usual in the time of Jesus first appears in the 'Psalms of Solomon' xvii, as above. (2) The name 'Son of Man', used for the Divine viceregent in I Enoch, clearly is adapted from Dan. vii (where it stands for Israel): the derivation, however, is plain, since both Daniel and I Enoch associate the Son of Man with God described as the 'Ancient of Days', and the general imagery is the same. (3) In I Enoch cv. 2 (probably second century B.C.) the Messiah is called the 'Son of God'. In II Sam. vii. 14 and Ps. lxxxix. 27 this is a name for the Davidic king: probably also in Ps. ii. 7, though the transference here to the Messiah was easy in view of the general tone of the Psalm. Anyhow, the name whether it stands for the Davidic king or the Messiah has a functional, not a metaphysical meaning. But again, the metaphysical sense was not distant, since the angels are called 'sons of God' in the Old Testament, as in Job xxxviii. 7. In IV Ezra (an Apocalypse of the first century A.D.) God speaks of 'my Son, the Messiah' (vii. 28–29); while in xiii. 25f. the same 'my Son' is a pre-existent Being, who is also called a Man. In the Hebrew of the Old Testament 'man' and 'son of man' were equivalents (Ps. viii. 4), so that IV Ezra brings together both the 'Son of God' and 'Son of Man' descriptions of the pre-existent Messiah.

We have still to consider Jewish thought about the Spirit. In the Old Testament the Spirit (*ruach*) is primarily a power that comes from God upon man, enabling him to do extraordinary and supernatural acts. A general outpouring of the Spirit is a mark of the future age. In Joel ii. 28 it produces prophecy, in Isa. xliv. 3f., Ezek. xi. 19, xxxvi. 26, religious regeneration. In Isa. xi. 2 it is the endowment of the Messiah. The name, 'spirit', however, was also used for spiritual beings subordinate to God (I Sam. xviii. 10; I Kings xxii. 19f.). In the later Judaism such beings were commonly spoken of as angels: after the exile apparently under Babylonian and Persian influence there was a great development of angelology, which is specially evident in the Apocalyptic literature. Finally, Isa. xxxi. 3 implies that God Himself is Spirit; and in Ps. li. 11 and Isa. lxiii. 10 the Spirit is called holy.

We are now in a position to study the *kerygma* of Acts. As indicated previously, we take first the four speeches

to Jews: ii. 14–36, 38, 39, iii. 12–26, iv. 3–12, v. 29–32.
We note that in the New Testament the name Messiah
is literally translated as Christ (Χριστός), also meaning
'Anointed'.

The very first of Peter's speeches contains all the
starting-points of the doctrine of the Trinity. Peter says
that the 'speaking with tongues' which had broken out
in the Christian assembly had resulted from the outpouring of the Spirit prophesied by Joel (ii. 28–32). It is
David's descendant Jesus, raised from the dead and
exalted to God's right hand who has poured out the
Spirit, the promised gift of God the Father. He, a man
approved of God by mighty works and wonders and
signs, has been wickedly crucified; but God has raised him
up, and has made Him both Lord and Christ. Salvation
in the day of the Messianic judgment, beginning with the
remission of sins, is ensured by repentance and baptism
in His name.

Here we have God the Father, Jesus the Christ and the
Spirit all together. If we supplement the first speech
from the others, we see that God is described as the God
of Abraham, Isaac and Jacob, 'the God of our fathers'
(ii. 13). In other words, we begin with Jewish monotheism.
The Spirit witnesses to the truth of the *kerygma*, v. 32.
But the central point of all the speeches is already contained in the phrase, 'God has made Him both Lord and
Christ, this Jesus whom ye crucified'. It is especially in
the title 'Lord' that the primitive *kerygma* verges towards
Trinitarianism. But not very far. It has been pointed out
indeed that in the same speech (Acts ii) the Apostle
quotes from Joel, 'Whosoever shall call upon the name of
the Lord shall be saved', where 'the Lord' is just a paraphrase for JAHWEH, in other words means God. But the
closer explanatory reference in Acts ii. 34–36 is to Ps. cx.
1, where the Hebrew gives us 'JAHWEH said unto Adoni',
so that the Greek translation, εἶπεν κύριος τῷ κυρίῳ μου,

means properly in Peter's mouth, 'the Lord God said to the Lord Messiah', where God and His viceregent are clearly distinguished; as indeed the context shows, continuing: 'Sit thou on my right hand till I make thine enemies the footstool of thy feet.' Still in Hebrew at that time the text was read as 'Adonai said to Adoni', and the same word κύριος is used for both God and the Messiah in Greek. Also if it is those who call on the name of God in the day of Judgment that will be saved, they are baptized in the saving name of His Representative, Jesus (cp. Acts ii. 38 with iv. 12). Jesus in fact stands in the place of God as Saviour, bestowing repentance and forgiveness (v. 31: cp. Mk. ii. 7, where the scribes say, 'Who can forgive sins, but God only?') To sum up, God and the Messiah are brought together by the use of the same name and the same saving function, but as yet are clearly distinguished. The whole point of Peter's speech is that it is the man, Jesus of Nazareth, known to his hearers, who has been made Lord Messiah, the viceregent of God.

Two comments are here necessary. One is addressed to the theological left. Against the assertion that the title 'Lord' is Hellenistic and could not be Palestinian stands the Aramaic *Marana tha* (Our Lord come) preserved by Paul in I Cor. xvi. 22, clear evidence of the use of the title in the Aramaic speaking Palestinian church. But there is danger of going wrong also on the theological right: the second comment is that it will not do to say with Cullmann that all the New Testament writers presuppose the same 'Christ-line' from pre-existence to Second Coming, but that it is mostly presented only in a fragmentary way (*Christ and Time*, pp. 108ff.) On the contrary, in Peter's speeches there is no hint of pre-existence: we are far from 'The Word became flesh'. Peter goes back no further than Jesus, the son of David. His conception of the Messiah, however, corresponds exactly to neither of the Jewish anticipations above described, any more

B

than it agrees precisely with later New Testament doctrine. It is New Testament theology in the making, original and important, but only a beginning and no more.

Are we to say that it is 'adoptianist'? By adoptianism in the history of Christology is meant the doctrine that Jesus was a man who by the grace of God lived a perfectly holy life, and so merited to be raised to Divine rank. Peter's *kerygma* is not adoptianist, because the thought of merit is not in his mind any more than that of pre-existence. All we can say is that when the controversy arose between adoptianism and incarnationism, it was natural for the adoptianists to appeal to Acts in support of their views: they could, like Cullmann, assume that more was implied than was mentioned, only they asserted a different implication.

There is just one more point to be observed before we leave the first four Petrine speeches. This has to do with the Spirit, which is chiefly spoken of impersonally as a power bestowed; but the mention of witness (Acts v. 32) suggests personality, and carries us some way towards Trinitarianism, though not very far as yet.

We still have to deal with the very remarkable speech to Cornelius, Acts x. 34–43. Here we see how the primitive *kerygma* was adopted to meet the needs of a Gentile 'God-fearer', that is one who without becoming a Jewish proselyte and submitting to circumcision, accepted monotheism and frequented the synagogue. For Cornelius the *kerygma* is expanded into a short sketch of the life of Jesus, ending with His appointment by God to be the Judge both of the living and the dead, and with the offer of forgiveness in His name.

The elementary outline of the life of Jesus is important as the germ from which the gospel story grew, and became what we find in Mark. There is an advance upon the former speeches of Peter, in that the Messiahship of

Jesus is carried back from His resurrection and subsequent exaltation to His baptism, when God anointed Him with Holy Spirit and with power. The anointing of course means the fitting of Jesus for the Messianic office. He is then depicted as a man living in fellowship with God ('God was with Him'), while an ethical turn is given to the description of His mighty works and wonders and signs, when it is said that He went about doing good and healing the demoniacs.

The archaic character of the speech to Cornelius is evident. Its Aramaic origin cannot be doubted. It is one more witness of the presence in the New Testament of a type of preaching which was not incarnational, but which began with the man Jesus of Nazareth, proclaiming him as Messiah. We have evidence in Acts x that such preaching could be extended even to Gentiles, as long as they had a sufficient sympathy with Judaism. It was different when men with a genuinely Hellenistic background were addressed by Paul. Then a second type of preaching became necessary, as we shall see presently.

Before, however, we go on to Paul, there is more to be said of the Palestinian Church. Although in Peter's speech to Cornelius there is the outline from which Mark's gospel was expanded, the church of Palestine itself produced no gospel. But it did produce a work of the highest importance, which modern criticism has revealed to us as the other source besides Mark of the gospels of Matthew and Luke. It is generally known as Q (German, *Quelle*, meaning 'source'). A convenient account of the presumed contents of Q is to be found in the article, 'The Synoptic Problem', by Streeter in Peake's *Commentary on the Bible*. The substance of Q is an account of the teaching of Jesus in a Messianic and eschatological framework: it appears to have been written as a manual of moral instruction for the Messianic community awaiting the advent of the Messiah from heaven. It is probably contemporary with the Pauline epistles, belonging to the period before the fall of Jerusalem in A.D. 70.

Q has a particular value for Christology, and therefore for the doctrine of the Trinity, in that it reminds us of the place occupied by teaching in the life and work of Jesus. This means that the miraculous healings, the crucifixion, and the resurrection, which form the content of the *kerygma*, only constitute the gospel because they refer to One whose character we know from His teaching. If the *kerygma* is the starting point of the later dogma, Q provides the basis of the religious-ethical view of Jesus in modern times.

It accords with the Apocalyptic character of the manual that in it the Messiah is called the 'Son of Man', as in Lk. xvii. 24, 26, 30. [References are given to Lk. rather than to Mt.: Lk. is generally considered to stand nearer to the original Q, where Lk. and Mt. differ.] It is noticeable that there is no suggestion of the pre-existence of the Son of Man, as in Enoch. The outlook is towards the future, as in Peter's speeches.

Light upon the character and inner life of Jesus comes from the story of the Temptation. Satan calls Him by the Messianic title, the Son of God; but He himself interprets it to mean dependence upon God. The Temptation is about the nature of Messiahship. Jesus will be no thaumaturge, no nationalist leader, thus dissevering Himself from current Jewish expectations. This is the more noteworthy, since the name 'Son of God' naturally connects itself with the Davidic prophecies of II Sam. vii. 14 and Ps. lxxxix. 20, 29. But Jesus connects Messiahship with his filial relation to God. In agreement with this we find a high point of Q in Lk. x. 21, 22, where Jesus addresses God, the Lord of heaven and earth as Father, and goes on to describe His unique filial relation to God and the authority He has from Him. It is possible that the form of x. 22, which seems like an anticipation

of the Johannine theology, may be *Gemeindedogmatik*,
Church theology. But there can be no doubt that it is
substantially true to the mind of Jesus Himself, as dis-
played in the story of the Temptation.

It is noteworthy further that in spite of the Apocalyptic
setting of Q, it records the teaching of Jesus that His
Messianic Kingdom is already realized in His miracles
and preaching (Lk. vii. 20f., xi. 20). His humanity too is
emphasized. Though He is 'Son of Man', he has no place
where to lay His head (Lk. ix. 58). His endowment with
the Spirit is also marked. He rejoices in the Holy Spirit
(Lk. x. 21).

A word may be added on the teaching which forms an
essential content of Q. Comparison with the Jewish
thought of the time only serves to illustrate its originality.
It discloses a unique mentality. The verdict recorded in
Jn. vii. 46 stands true, 'Never man so spake'. In its
religious-ethical character the teaching of Jesus stands
alone; and when we come to the story of His life in Mark
we find that life and teaching are one.

3. THE HELLENISTIC WORLD

The *kerygma* of the Petrine speeches represents the
Palestinian church on one side: its *didache* or teaching is
contained in Q. Together, they enable us to understand
Christianity in its original Jewish Christian form. The
greater part of the New Testament belongs, however, to
the Christianity of the Hellenistic world, where it was a
missionary religion. In moving from Palestine into this
larger sphere Christianity underwent a great transformation. To understand the nature of the change it is necessary
to comprehend the factors of the new situation. We have
to consider the religion of the Greco-Roman world in the
Apostolic age, and also have to pay some attention to
the prevalent philosophies.

It was a very religious age: cp. Acts xvii. 22. The first work of the Christian mission was to turn men from the worship of idols to that of the true God as a basis for the preaching of the risen Jesus (Acts xvii. 31; I Thess. i. 9, 10). The religion to be overcome was, firstly, that of the local cult, often by a syncretism characteristic of the period identified with one or other of the great gods of the Greek pantheon. Secondly, there was the Cæsar-worship accompanying the Roman empire. But, thirdly, there was another type of religion Oriental in origin, missionary in character, and like Christianity bringing a promise of salvation. This was the religion of the mysteries, in which the initiated put themselves under the protection of a particular divinity whom they voluntarily accepted as Lord and Saviour-God. Such Oriental mystery-religions were not tied to a particular spot like the ancient Eleusinian mysteries near Athens: they were spread as Christianity was spread by travelling preachers who took them everywhere. They were universalistic religions, entrance into which was independent of nationality and status. In the points mentioned, their soteriological, voluntary and universalistic character they run parallel with the Hellenistic Christianity described in the New Testament; and it is natural, that in spite of all differences there should be points of contact between the two.

One such point, which we shall find of importance later on, is the conception of the missionary preacher or wandering prophet as a Divine man, θεῖος ἄνθρωπος, who evidences his mission by working miracles. Such figures were often spoken of as 'sons of God'. The name was the old pagan title for the heroes who traditionally had a Divine father. But the nomenclature for the mystic prophet went even further. He was spoken of sometimes as a god, as coming from heaven, and as being sent into the world. The whole subject is exhaustively studied in Wetter's book, *Der Sohn Gottes* (1916). But the New

Testament itself offers most remarkable illustrations of the conception. One is that of Simon the sorcerer, who enjoyed the reputation of being 'that power of God which is called Great' (Acts viii. 10). Another is that of the reception of Paul and Barnabas at Lystra, when the crowds cried aloud, 'The gods are come down to us in the likeness of men' (Acts xiv. 11). Finally, there is the case of the heathen centurion, who was so impressed by the way that Jesus died that he said, 'Truly this man was a son of God' (Mk. xv. 39, R.V. marg).

Not only Hellenistic religion, but Hellenistic philosophy also affected the situation into which Christianity came. The reason was that the philosophy of the time was itself to a great extent religious in character. To begin with, the philosophic giants of the past, Plato and Aristotle, had left behind them a legacy conducive to theistic belief. The Platonic distinction between two worlds, one eternal and real, the other temporal and shadowy, had a natural affinity with the distinction between the Divine and the creaturely. Moreover, while Plato's fundamental philosophical principle was the Idea of the Good, in the *Timæus* he spoke of a Demiurge or Creator-God, and in memorable words at the end of the book, called the universe the Image of God and the visible God. Aristotle was even more definitely a theist of sorts: at the head of his metaphysical system he put a First Mover, whom he described as pure activity, and as the Thought that thinks itself.

But the philosophy which was most influential in the world into which Christianity came was Stoicism: more recent than Plato or Aristotle it was a great cultural force with a wide popular appeal. Just as there were wandering prophets, so also there were wandering philosophers, who diffused the Stoic philosophy everywhere as a cure for the ills of the time. Though the main interest of the Stoics was in ethics, they nevertheless gave their system a physical basis, and more than either Plato or

Aristotle had done they expressed their doctrine in theological terminology.

In their physics they were materialists. Everything was body, God included. But they distinguished a coarser and a finer matter. The latter was πνεῦμα, warm air, or alternatively fire, penetrating as a force through all things. Its effluences, the organizing powers of the world they called λόγοι σπερματικοί, seminal principles. The ancient philosopher, Heraclitus, from whom they borrowed the notion of fire as the dynamic principle of the universe, had spoken of Logos, world-reason as its divine law; but it has been denied recently that the Stoics so used Logos in the singular. They did, however, describe the reason of man as *logos*, distinguishing λόγος ἐνδιάθετος, reason immanent as inward thought, from λόγος προφορικός, reason uttered as outwardly spoken word. Altogether, Logos therefore with them is a term pregnant with meaning. It unites the notion of a natural principle with human reason and human word. The Stoics made it the basis of their ethics. To be virtuous was to live in agreement with nature (φύσις), or in other words to follow reason.

When the Stoics spoke theologically they identified the original fire or *pneuma* with God, who was in one the material and the dynamic principle of the world, whence all emanates and into which all returns. Inasmuch as all proceeds according to law, the Stoics described the world-process as providence, which however was just another name for fate. But they used religious language freely. God was λογικός, rational, τέλειος, perfect, and was called πατήρ πάντων, the Father of all things. The constant use of religious language does indeed show that the Stoics in spite of their fundamental materialism, thought religiously and valued religion. Their monism in fact became a pantheism. This enabled them to find a place in their system for the gods of the popular religion, which older philosophers like Xenophanes and Plato had criticized. They viewed them as subordinate beings, identifiable with the stars and with the forces of nature, but not sharing in the eternity of the Supreme Being. The anthropomorphism of the ancient religious myths was translated into philosophy by allegorization.

The mystery religions and the religious philosophy of Paganism, especially the Stoic philosophy, each in its way helped to prepare the path for Christianity as a missionary religion. But the great bridge after all over which the Christian religion passed into the Gentile world was that of Hellenistic Judaism. It was a form of Judaism which, while it retained the strictest monotheism and the strictest regard for the Mosaic law, had yet learned to speak so as to be intelligible to the Gentiles. The Jews were dispersed all over the Roman empire, and their religion had made many proselytes and adherents by its exalted monotheism and ethics.

Jewish thought was either scornful of the heathen divinities as 'things of nought' (Is. xliv. 9f.; Ps. cxv), or else it abominated them as demons (Deut. xxxii. 17; Ps. cvi. 37, and the Apocalyptic literature in general). The latter view joins up with the exuberant development of angelology which marks the post-exilic period. For the demons were simply angels who had gone wrong (Gen. vi. 2). Other angels were valued as God's ministers to do His pleasure (Ps. ciii. 20–21). The need of such intermediaries between God and the World was felt because of the post-exilic increasing sense of the absolute transcendence of God, which required that there should be substitutes even for His name, as has been mentioned already.

It will be observed that the relation of the angels to JAHWEH is not so altogether unlike that of the subordinate divinities to the Supreme Being in the Stoic philosophy. The resemblance to Greek thought is even more marked, when we consider the very remarkable Jewish doctrine of *hypostasis*. This word is used in modern Biblical theology, without prejudice to its use in the doctrine of the Trinity, to mean an attribute or operation of God, raised to a certain degree of independence and often described in personal terms. The ancient world had not our conception of personality as self-consciousness, and the margin between what we distinguish as personal and impersonal was indistinct. The word 'hypostasis' meant originally simply 'substance' (as in Heb. xi. 1, R.V.): its peculiar use in the doctrine of the Trinity will be examined in due course.

The most important of the Jewish hypostases for our present study are those of the Divine Word, the Divine Spirit and the Divine Wisdom. The first two ideas are less developed in the Old Testament than the last. But all have the same purpose, viz. to mediate between God and the Creation. A particularly notable passage is Ps. xxxiii. 6: 'By the word of the Lord were the heavens made, and all the host of them by the breath of His mouth.' Here the Hebrew word *ruach*, translated 'breath' is the same as is frequently translated 'spirit'. The Greek *pneuma* and the Latin *spiritus* have similarly both senses. From the above passage we see that 'word' and 'spirit' are used as equivalents: this is plain because of the parallelism of Hebrew poetry in which two clauses mean the same, though differently expressed. The hypostatization of 'word' comes out very clearly in Ps. cxlvii. 15–18, and that of 'spirit' in Ps. civ. 30. The 'word' runs; the 'word' and the 'spirit' are sent.

Such hypostatization, however, pales before that of the Divine Wisdom, as we have it in 'Proverbs' and even more strikingly in the 'Wisdom of Solomon' in the Apocrypha. In Prov. viii. 22 Wisdom is spoken of as the coadjutor of God in the work of creation, and also as the friend and guide of man. In Wisd. vii. 22f. the description is more philosophical, and is drawn out at great length.

There is in Wisdom an intellectual and holy spirit, unique (literally only-begotten, μονογενές), beneficent and loving towards men, pervading not only all spirits, but indeed all things. She is further an effluence (ἀπόρροια) of the glory of the Almighty, an effulgence (ἀπαύγασμα) from everlasting light, and an image (εἰκών) of God's goodness. And from generation to generation passing into holy souls, she makes men friends of God and prophets.

In his *Theologie des alten Testaments*, II, p. 44, Eichrodt has pointed out the importance of the Jewish conception of wisdom in its approximation to Greek thought. For the Jews the law contained the knowledge of God and of nature as well as ethical instruction; so that it was possible to give an answer to the questions raised in Greek philosophy without leaving the firm ground of Revelation. Prov. viii. 22f. (300–250 B.C.) is a most remarkable first effort in this direction. But when we come to Wisd. viii. 22f. (first century B.C.), though the thought continues to be Jewish, there are plain signs of the direct influence of the Stoic terminology. Judæa and Greece are met together, and the Hebrew Wisdom is identified with the Stoic *pneuma*.

The 'Wisdom of Solomon' also contains a rational proof of monotheism and disproof of polytheism. In Wisd. xiii. 1f. idolatry is traced to the failure of the heathen world to rise beyond the works of God in creation, which they falsely deified, to God Himself as their creator.

The final stage in the approximation of Jewish and Greek thought is found in the philosophy of Philo, an Alexandrian contemporary of both Jesus and Paul. In Alexandria in the first century B.C. there had arisen an eclectic philosophy which was even more religiously disposed than Stoicism—under the name of Neo-Pythagoreanism and in touch with the mystery religions, it had absorbed elements from Plato, Aristotle and the Stoics, converting the whole into a religious metaphysic. It was in connection with the ideas of this eclecticism that

Philo undertook to complete the work of mediating between Greek and Hebrew thought. His intention was to present Judaism in a form intelligible to the Hellenistic world. He allegorized the Old Testament as the Greeks had allegorized their own mythology.

Philo begins with God, concerning Whom the only positive statement that can be made is that He is. Beyond this nothing at all can be said. The Jewish philosopher is at one with the Neo-Pythagoreans in emphasizing the Divine transcendence. God is unknowable and indescribable. Nevertheless, there is a bridge between God and the world. This is the Divine Logos, who contains in himself all the immanent principles of the Universe. These principles Philo calls not only ideas, powers and reasons (λόγοι), but also angels and demons. We note how easy is the transition from the abstract philosophical conception to the concrete and personalized existence.

The Logos is called the firstborn Son of God, begotten of God. He beholds in God the archetypes of being, and imitates His ways. In saying that the Logos is begotten (γεννηθείς), Philo intends to fix his position between God who is unoriginate (ἀγένητος) and man who is originate (γενητός). His relation to mankind is that of an Archangel, their original pattern in the Divine image. Philo goes so far as to call him a second God. It will be remembered that Plato had spoken of the universe as a visible God.

The Logos is further described as the representative of men before God, our High Priest, who supplicates for the corruptible before the Incorruptible. The question is usually asked: In this hypostatization of the Logos did Philo conceive the Logos personally or impersonally? The common answer is that his conception was impersonal. But we have seen that the question does not properly arise, the ancient world not having our distinct notion of personality. There is more to be said on the point, which is one of great importance for our further study of the

New Testament. The whole conception of the hypostases in Jewish theology in general is altogether fluctuating. The hypostasis was introduced simply to show how the transcendent God could act in the world without losing His transcendence. We have seen that 'word' and 'spirit' can be used quite interchangeably for this purpose (Ps. xxxiii. 6). And Eichrodt says (*loc. cit., supra*) that Jewish teachers never succeeded in fixing the relation between God's 'word' and His 'wisdom'. In fact they alternate: all that one can say is that they connote different aspects of the same activity. A further and very striking proof of the fluctuating character of the hyposta-tization of God's attributes and operations is to be seen in the fact that the figure of wisdom in Jewish theology is feminine in agreement with the gender of *Chokmah* the Hebrew word for wisdom: the Greek σοφιά preserves the same gender in translation. On the other hand the Hebrew *Dabhar*, word, is masculine; as also its equivalent, the Greek λόγος, so that Philo can speak consistently of the Logos as a High Priest. All this helps to show how unsafe it is to argue that any of the hypostases imply personality in the modern sense of the word. Moreover, Jewish theologians used the hypostases without intending any infringement of their monotheism. It has been well said that JAHWEH, in contrast with the gods of polytheism, had neither wife nor child. (The point is well brought out in Köhler's *Theologie des Alten Testaments*, pp. 2ff.) The hypostases were never meant to alter this fundamental position. And yet it is said in Wisd. viii. 3 that wisdom glorifies her noble birth in that it is given to her to live with God, and that God loves her, and in ix. 4 that wisdom sits by God on His throne.

4. THE PAULINE EPISTLES

The foregoing long survey of Hellenistic religion and thought ending with the consideration of Hellenistic

Judaism was necessary if we are to understand the change which Christianity underwent in passing out from Palestine into the Greco-Roman world. The Christians of Jerusalem, while proclaiming Jesus, risen from the dead, to be the Messiah promised to Israel, all the same continued to observe the Mosaic law and joined in the temple-worship. Thus, in spite of their baptism in the name of Jesus, they seemed to be little more than a Jewish sect.

A break with Judaism came when Stephen, a Hellenistic Jew, declared that the observance of the law was no longer incumbent upon Christians; and from this time a Hellenistic form of Christianity developed with great rapidity. Its centre was at Antioch, where the distinction from Judaism was clearly recognized: we are told in Acts xi. 26 that the disciples were first called 'Christians' there.

Together with this new Hellenistic Christianity, there grew up a theology appropriate to it. The New Testament contains several different examples of this theology. The oldest form in which it has come down to us is in the Epistles of Paul. No doubt Paul had predecessors: he appears to treat much of his Christology in particular as already known to and accepted by those to whom he writes, and then proceeds to draw out its ethical consequences. It is thought, for example, that in Phil. ii. 5–11, he may be quoting from a Christian hymn already in use. But for our purposes it will suffice to deal with the contents of the epistles as 'Pauline theology': whatever Paul accepted from others he made his own, and the whole comes down to us with the stamp of his astonishing personality upon it.

In studying Paul we may make use of practically everything we have under his name, except of course the Epistle to the Hebrews which is clearly not Pauline, and the Pastoral Epistles which, even if they have a Pauline basis, reflect a later situation than that of the Apostle. Colossians is now very commonly regarded as Pauline, and Ephesians stands so near to it that even if it is the work of a Pauline disciple, it can be included in a survey of Paulinism. As to II Thessalonians, whether it is Pauline or not, it contains nothing for our purpose which is not found elsewhere. The Pauline Epistles belong to the fifties and sixties of the first Christian century.

The general intention of Paul was to universalize Christianity, as is most clearly to be seen from the Epistle to the Romans, where he has set out the salient points of his understanding of the gospel. We noted the absence from the original *kerygma* of the clause in the Pauline version of it, 'that Christ died for our sins according to the Scriptures'. This addition to the *kerygma* became the very centre of the Apostle's preaching (I Cor. ii. 2): thus, while preserving the expectation of the Messianic advent, he completely altered the evangelical emphasis, which now fell not upon what Christ would do in the future, but upon what He had done in the past and upon the present blessings enjoyed by the Christian.

There is here a parallel with what Q also did about the same time by reviving the words of Jesus about the Kingdom as already present, and about the beatitude of those who belong to it (Lk. x. 23, 24). Paul himself similarly writes of the Kingdom in Rom. xiv. 17. No doubt the delay of the Messianic advent worked to the same end in both cases.

But the parallel with Q ends when we consider how in Q the past work of Jesus is represented as above all one of teaching, while Paul concentrates all that He did into His birth, death and resurrection, especially the last two. It is by means of Christ's death and resurrection that he has interpreted anew the Messianic gifts of forgiveness and the Holy Spirit offered on condition of repentance and baptism by Peter. Paul translates forgiveness (Rom.

iv. 6–8) into its equivalent, justification from the condemnation of the law, not grounded upon any meritorious
works, but established by Christ's death and resurrection,
and to be received by faith in Him. In this way the
Apostle provides a theological basis for the freedom from
the law proclaimed by Stephen. As regards the other
Messianic gift, that of the Holy Spirit, the transformation
is equally remarkable. This also is now deduced from
Christ's death and resurrection, but by a different method.
They are treated as inclusive acts, which translate those
united to Christ by faith and baptism into the new life of
the Spirit, which is one of filial trust in God's Fatherhood,
of active righteousness, and of the assured hope of
immortality.

Paul has succeeded in unifying his whole doctrine of
justification by faith and the gift of the Holy Spirit by
means of the important conception of the 'second man'
(or Second Adam), for which we have to go not only to
Romans, but also to I Corinthians to complete the view.
According to Rom. v. 12f. Christ as the Second and
sinless Adam by His righteous act in dying undid the
condemnation passed by the law upon the race of the
first and sinful Adam; while according to I Cor. xv. 22,
45f. by His resurrection He became a life-giving spirit
and changed man's penal state of mortality into one of
immortality. We have here a point of view destined to
bear great fruit in the later history of Christian doctrine.

In its Pauline form the gospel has been completely
universalized. Jew and Greek both are descended from
Adam, and Paul preaches equally to both. As a preliminary to so doing he universalizes the knowledge of
God and His law. He follows the 'Wisdom of Solomon' in
arguing that God may be known from the order of the
created world, and that idolatry is folly and worse (Rom.
i. 18f.). Nor does he disdain to utilize the Stoic idea of the
law of reason immanent in every man and acting in his

conscience (Rom. ii. 14f.). It is noteworthy that the Apostle, in spite of his doctrine of justification by faith, does not abandon that of a future judgment (ii. 16), which is to be according to works (II Cor. v. 10). We have here a complete set of ideas, (1) the universal knowledge of God and His law, with (2) judgment according to works, and (3) immortality as the reward of obedience; taken as a whole they are of great importance for the later development of doctrine.

To come back, however, to the Pauline universalized gospel, it naturally required a universalized Christology sufficient to carry it, and equal to supporting the view of Christ as the Second Adam. This we have now to study: it is on the great scale. But it is essential to see that Paul presents the whole of his elaborate theological gospel as an expansion of the original *kerygma*. Rom. i. 1–4 in fact might appear at first sight to be simply a repetition of it. Jesus Christ is the Son of God, promised in prophecy, of the stock of David, whose spirit is holy, and who has been established as Son of God by the resurrection, and so is our Lord. Here almost every element in the description corresponds to a point of the Petrine *kerygma*. And yet there is a change implied. First of all, Christ (or Messiah) has become simply a proper name. Paul uses 'Jesus Christ' and 'Christ Jesus' alternatively, in this way. 'Messiah' had not the same great significance for a Gentile that it had for a Jew; and so what it meant to the Jew had to find a Gentile equivalent. The name Lord already used by the Palestinian church supplied one form of such equivalent. The heathen had 'gods many and lords many' as saving divinities: the meaning of the Messiahship of Jesus was translated for them by saying that while there was no God but One, so there was only One Lord (I Cor. viii. 4–6). Yet another way of translating Messiahship was to say that Jesus Christ was the Son of God. To a Jew the names Messiah and Son of God were

c

synonyms; because, as we have seen, Son of God was the name of the ideal Davidic king. But to a Gentile 'Son of God' brought all the associations of the Divine man, come down from heaven and manifest on earth, a conception not so far removed from the other Jewish Messianic belief in a Messiah pre-existent with God. It is not clear whether Paul had thought of the Messiah in this latter way before his conversion, or whether he found the belief in the pre-existent Son of God already established in the Hellenistic Christianity into which he came at Antioch. What is perfectly clear is that both for him and Hellenistic Christianity in general Christ was the pre-existent Son of God, and that the Christians of Jerusalem, while differing from Paul over his gospel, never criticized his Christology.

When we look again at Rom. i. 1–4 we see that Jesus Christ stands as Son of God even before He is declared to be so with power. Moreover, He is not described as 'anointed with Holy Spirit'; as Son of God, His spirit is one of holiness. These are subtle changes, but their reason is made plain in other passages in which the doctrine of pre-existence becomes ever clearer and fuller till we reach a culminating point in Phil. ii. 5–11. In I Cor. x. 4 we read that Christ was already with the Israelites in the wilderness, so that God's sending of His Son (Gal. iv. 4 and Rom. viii. 3) is not the beginning of His life, but a transition from heavenly glory to the indigence of earthly existence (II Cor. viii. 9), which theme Phil. ii. 5–11 develops at length. Whether Paul is using an already existing hymn or not does not really matter: we have the passage as one of the key-points of the Apostle's theology.

It is said that Christ Jesus, being in the form of God, instead of grasping at equality with God, emptied Himself, taking the form of a servant and being made in the likeness of men. In this state He further humbled Himself in obedience to God to the death of the Cross, for which

cause God exalted Him to a universal Lordship. This
Lordship is illustrated from Isa. xlv. 23, where the prophet
speaks of the sovereignty of JAHWEH. But the application
of the quotation to Christ is limited by the declaration
that the confession of His Lordship is to be to the glory
of God the Father.

Upon this great passage some comments must now be
made. What is peculiarly interesting and important is
that in it the original *kerygma* is set in an Incarnational
framework. The *kerygma* stands out with remarkable
clearness, with the adoptianist motive, before lacking,
now definitely supplied. The key-word here is 'wherefore'
(διό) in ii. 9, which introduces the principle of merit: it
was by His obedience in dying that Christ merited
Lordship. Moreover, monotheism is emphasized; His
Lordship is confessed to the glory of the Father.

And now the Incarnational framework. The first point
to be noted is that a humiliation upon earth is reduplicated
by a humiliation in heaven. Such reduplication is in
accordance with a principle well known in Jewish and
Jewish Christian theology. In Dan. x. 19–20 the struggles
of the nations have their heavenly counterpart; while in
Rev. xii. 7, 8, 13, 17 the same is true of the conflicts of
the Christian martyrs. There is a parallel in the modern
doctrine that the sacrifice of Jesus on the Cross was the
revelation of an eternal sacrifice in the heart of God,
reference being made to Rev. xiii. 8, 'the Lamb, slain
from the foundation of the world'.

As to the humiliation of the Incarnation, not much
is to be discovered with regard to what is meant, simply
by an exhaustive study of the terms used, μορφή, form,
in the phrases 'form of God' and 'form of a servant',
and ὁμοίωμα, likeness, and σχῆμα, fashion, with
reference to Christ's humanity. According to Dibelius
in the *Handbuch zum neuen Testament* (in loc.) all these
terms, though of philosophical origin are here employed

just as words in common use, and their meaning is to be taken from the context. The general thought is that of a heavenly being, who however is not equal to God. But unlike Adam in Gen. ii. 5, the King of Babylon in Isa. xiv. 13, and the Prince of Tyre in Ezek. xxviii. 2, Christ Jesus does not grasp at equality with God, but takes the way of humility, and is rewarded with the title of Lord, which apparently He had not before; just as in Rom. i. 1–4 He was from the first Son of God, but not Son of God 'with power'.

Neither here or elsewhere in the New Testament is there any explanation of the mode of the Incarnation, any more than there is any explicit doctrine of the Trinity. All that was to follow from reflection upon the primitive charismatic expression of Christianity.

We have now studied two ways in which the Apostle Paul reinterpreted the Messiahship of Jesus for the Gentile world. One was, Jesus is Lord (I Cor. xii. 3); the other, Jesus is the Son of God (cp. Acts ix. 20). Both were charismatic confessions, which appear to have arisen spontaneously out of the ambivalence of the terms 'Lord' and 'Son of God': they had, as we may say, a two-way character implying to a Jewish mind Messiahship, but to a Gentile mind a wider connotation. Paul uses both; but these forms of confession may well be as old as Hellenistic Christianity in its pre-Pauline beginnings. They were universal in the Gentile Church, nor did the Church of Jerusalem take exception to them. Their charismatic character is clearly indicated in I Cor. xii. 3 and I Jn. iv. 13–15.

There is yet another form of Pauline Christology. It was a Christology in which Christ, the pre-existent Son of God, is identified with the cosmic Wisdom or the Logos (though Paul never actually uses the latter term). The full development of this Christology was occasioned by Paul's resistance to the angel worship which was invading the church of Colossæ, but it is clear that the conception existed seminally in his mind at an earlier date. He had universalized Jewish monotheism by adopting the arguments of the 'Wisdom of Solomon' (Rom. i. 18ff., Wisd. xiii. 1f.) what more natural than the universal Lordship of Christ should be involved in the very plan of the universe? We see Paul beginning so to write it into the method of the creation in I Cor. viii. 6. Other passages which point in the same direction are I Cor. i. 30 and II Cor. iv. 4 which speak of Christ as Wisdom from God and the Image of God; while in I Cor. xi. 3 He is said to be the head of every man. To identify the pre-existent Christ with the cosmic Wisdom was not difficult in view of the quasi-personal character of hypostases. Philo equates the Logos with an Archangel, and in general the line between angelic powers and abstract principles was very tenuous.

Paul, and others, therefore were thinking along such lines even before the angel-worship at Colossæ set in motion in his mind the process which produced the astonishing cosmic Christology of Col. i and ii. The Colossian heresy was clearly an incipient form of the Gnosticism which came to a head in the second century. It is necessary here to anticipate the account of that Gnosticism, so far as it throws light upon the trouble at Colossæ. The great concern of all Gnosticism was with the problem of evil, which it solved by means of a dualism which sharply separated God as good from matter as evil.

To mediate between God and matter the Gnostics introduced a whole series of semi-divine powers. One form of Gnosticism spoke of a series of æons which constituted the fulfilment or completion (πλήρωμα) of God (cp. Col. ii. 9). Others brought in angels, which they regarded as the rulers of the present world. The pre-existent Christ was given a place among those spiritual beings, His principal work being to bring to men *Gnosis*, or knowledge of God and of the scheme of things, and so to free them from matter and the rule of subordinate powers. In this way there was salvation out of this evil world (cp. Gal. i. 4), at least for some. Asceticism was commonly inculcated as a means of deliverance from the power of matter.

The Colossian heretics appear to have had ideas very similar to those just described. They identified the angelic powers with the fundamental principles of the universe (στοιχεῖα, Col. ii. 20): as we have seen, continually in contemporary thought abstract and concrete easily interchange. By means of worship and ascetic practices they sought the protection of these powers (Col. ii. 20f.). What place they gave to Christ we do not know for certain, but there can be little doubt that they regard Him in His pre-existence as an angel along with the others.

It is clear that the Lordship of Christ was endangered. And to say that he was the Son of God was not enough; for the angels also were 'sons of God' (Gen. vi. 2; Job i. 6, ii. 1, xxxviii. 7). Paul had certainly intended to convey the uniqueness of Christ's Divine Sonship, when he called Him God's own Son (Rom. viii. 3). Colossæ overlooked such teaching.

To meet the difficulty Paul develops the doctrine of Christ as the cosmic Wisdom in Col. i and ii on a scale that transcends the cosmos itself. He shared with the Colossian heretics the general view which equated the elementary principles of the universe with spiritual beings such as not only the pagan divinities, but also the angels who gave the Jewish law (Gal. iii. 19, iv. 8, 9). But he disallows not only all worship of the angels, but also the ascetism that tried to imitate the angelic life. For all such spiritual beings are subordinated to Christ, as indeed Paul had constantly maintained (I Cor. xv. 24f.), and as he now reasserts in new form (Col. ii. 14, 15). What Paul now says is that it was so from the very beginning (Col. i. 15–20, ii. 9, 10). Christ is said to be the Image of the invisible God, the firstborn of all creation. In Him all things were created, both earthly and visible, and heavenly and invisible. He is before all things and in Him all things consist. Moreover, in Him dwells all the fulness (πλήρωμα) of the Godhead bodily, and He is the Head of all principality and power; in other words, of the whole hierarchy of angels. And as the firstborn from the dead He is the Head of the Church, having the pre-eminence in all things. The parallel with Philippians ii at this point is striking. In both cases the Apostle begins with Christ's pre-existence, though he describes it in different ways. In both cases he comes back to the same ending, which is the original *kerygma* of a Lord-ship based on the Resurrection (Col. i. 18–20; cp. Phil. ii. 10).

Col. ii. 3 shows that the Apostle conceived his doctrine as a Gnosis opposed to the heretical Gnosis. He has written Jesus Christ into the scheme of the universe. He has universalized Christianity on the same scale as Philo universalized Judaism. There is no need to assume a direct relation between them. They shared the same intellectual atmosphere. But Philo began from the Mosaic law. Paul began from Jesus Christ.

In Colossians there appears to be some advance beyond the subordinationism which is very apparent in I Corinthians. I Cor. xi. 3 says that the head of Christ is God (cp. iii. 23); while I Cor. viii. 8 says that all things are of God and we unto Him, but only that all things are through Christ and we through Him. Still more marked is the subordinationism in I Cor. xv. 24–28, which speaks of Christ's final handing over of the Kingdom to the Father, and of His subjection to Him, that God may be all in all. In Colossians however, a change seems to begin. Certainly to speak of Christ as the firstborn of creation still has a subordinationist ring. But in i. 16 we read that all things are not

only through Christ, but also unto Him. If we bring in
Eph. v. 3, we are taken still further: instead of the final
subjection of Christ to God we have the eternal inheritance
spoken of as the Kingdom of Christ and God. But it is
not safe to argue too much from these changes. In Phil.
ii. 5–11 subordinationism is manifest in that Christ is
thought of as not originally equal to God, and even the
confession of Him as universal Lord is to the glory of
God the Father. It should be added that Rom. ix. 6
cannot be adduced to prove that Paul ever thought of
Christ as God. The state of the case is shown in the
R.V. margin.

Although Philippians is perhaps a little later than
Colossians (and also than Ephesians, if that is Pauline),
the Christology of Philippians is probably in essence the
earlier form of doctrine as compared with the cosmic
Christology of Colossians. If in Phil. ii. 5–11 Paul was
using an early Christian hymn that would substantially
prove the case, but anyhow the 'Son of God' Christology
is almost certainly as old as Hellenistic Christianity,
while the 'Wisdom' Christology was apparently a Pauline
creation occasioned by the Colossian heresy. We have
seen, however, that the principles of both types of
Christology were in Paul's mind when he wrote I Corinthians. Logically, at any rate, the cosmic Christology
seems to follow on the other, and not *vice versa*.

We pass on to Paul's doctrine of the Holy Spirit. It is
less developed than his Christology. But it is marked by
an important departure from the ancient Hebrew conception of a power that comes upon a man only occasionally. Paul thinks of the Spirit as a permanent regenerating
influence received by faith and baptism. The operation
of the Spirit is most truly seen, not in abnormal pheno-
mena, but in its ethical results (I Cor. xii. 1-xiii. 13;
Gal. v. 22). The Spirit is also a principle of sonship to

God (Rom. viii. 15; Gal. iv. 6) and an earnest of immortality (Rom. viii. 23; Eph. i. 14).

Paul mostly speaks of the Spirit as a gift, just as does
the original *kerygma*. But there are passages where there
is a more personal description of the Spirit, as I Cor. ii.
10, 11, 13, and notably Rom. viii. 16–27; cp. also Eph. iv.
30. However, in the same verse I Cor. ii. 11 where Paul
speaks of the Spirit in personal terms, he also compares
the relation of the Spirit of God to God with that of the
immanent spirit of man to man himself. The description
fluctuates.

In one passage the Apostle identifies Christ and the
Spirit (II Cor. iii. 17): apart from this direct identification
Paul elsewhere, as in Rom. viii. 9–11, speaks alternatively
of the indwelling Christ and the indwelling Spirit, and he
indifferently uses the names, 'the Spirit of God', 'the
Spirit of Christ', and 'the Spirit' simply, so that all these
terms slide into one another and become indistinguishable.
Reference has been made already in another context to
I Cor. xv. 45, where Paul says that the Second Adam
became a life-giving spirit. There was much fluidity in
the Apostle's thought.

It may be remarked further that πνεῦμα, spirit, had
for Hellenistic Christians not only a meaning based on
the Old Testament, but also that associated with the
Stoic philosophy, which was the notion of a subtle element
universally pervasive. Paul himself may well have been
influenced, as in other matters, by Stoicism as well as
by the Old Testament. He certainly did not live in a
hermetically sealed Hebraism at Tarsus or Antioch.
He became all things to all men, that he might by all
means save some. One aspect of his universalism is to be
seen in his use of ambivalent terms, words with a two-way
meaning. Some modern scholars see nothing but Hebraism
in Paul, others have their eyes only on what is Hellenistic.
Paul's theology has both aspects. It is like the famous

shield, white on one side, black on the other, over which two knights fought, one saying it was white, the other black.

In studying Paul's contribution to the doctrine of the Trinity, one final question remains to us. What is the reaction of all the foregoing theological development upon his doctrine of God?

In correspondence with his doctrine of the Sonship of Christ Paul continually speaks of God as the Father. But though he speaks of Christ as God's 'own Son' (Rom. viii. 3), while we are sons by adoption (Rom. viii. 13), yet he never leaves the ground of Jewish monotheism. It has been pointed out that Rom. ix. 5 cannot be brought in to question this statement. On the contrary, God is spoken of by the Apostle as not only the Father, but also the God of our Lord Jesus Christ (II Cor. i. 3; Eph. i. 17): the Ephesians reference is particularly noteworthy in an epistle where the subordination of Christ to God is otherwise lessened.

As to the relation of the Spirit to God, on the one hand God sends the Spirit (Gal. iv. 6); but on the other the Spirit is said to be the repository of all Divine knowledge and, as has been already noted, to be in God as the spirit of man is in man (I Cor. ii. 10, 11). Here is the one approach to a metaphysic of the Divine Being that we find in the Pauline Epistles.

Paul's monotheism finds direct expression in Gal. iii. 20, where he says, 'God is one', and even more definitely in I Cor. viii. 4: cp. also Eph. iv. 5. The one God is the Creator (Rom. i. 25), whose sovereignty is so tremendously affirmed in Rom. ix.-xi. His relation to the universe is summed up in the language of current Hellenistic philosophy, 'Of Him and through Him and unto Him are all things' (Rom. xi. 36): cp. also Eph. iv. 6, 'One God and Father of all, who is over all, and through all, and in all'. Transcendence and immanence are both implied.

Paul's transformation of the original *kerygma* in order to universalize it is the greatest turning point in Christian theology. It changed the original confession, Jesus is the Messiah, into its converse, the Son of God has taken the form of Jesus. Barth has well said that there are two Christologies in the New Testament; one, Jesus is the Son of God; the other, the Son of God is Jesus (*Kirchliche Dogmatik*, I, 2, p. 17). But the name Son of God does not mean just the same in both cases. In the first case it means the Messiah, in the second a pre-existent Being. We have seen how the one meaning could pass into the other, because the name continued the same.

In studying the original *kerygma*, it was said that Peter's first speech contains all the elements of Trinitarian doctrine, God the Father, Christ the Lord, and the Holy Spirit. But it does not contain them in such a way as to make a doctrine of the Trinity necessary. The necessity began when Paul universalized and transformed the *kerygma*. The fundamental problems of Christology and of the doctrine of the Trinity then arose: wherever the Pauline Epistles might be accepted as authoritative together with the Old Testament and the *kerygma*, two great questions would emerge, Could monotheism be preserved? and, Could justice be done to the humanity of Christ? These problems indeed were for a future date. Paul himself saw no problems. The charismatic character of his theology prevented them arising in his mind. Besides, as we have seen, he continually emphasizes the unity of God and the subordination of Christ to the Father; and as regards the humanity of Jesus it was enough for him that He was born of a woman, born under the law, and that He became obedient to the death of the cross (Gal. iv. 4; Phil. ii. 8): here was the centre not only of his gospel, but also of his personal religion (I Cor. ii. 2; Gal. ii. 20). Besides, it is most noteworthy that, just as he had developed his theology from the *kerygma* (Rom. i. 1–4), so after the whole development he could come back to it, and find it an all-sufficient confession of Christian faith (Rom. x. 9).

But the problems were there all the same, and the subsequent history of Christian theology has largely been occupied with dealing with them. Paul did not say that Christ was God, but he did say that He was originally in the form of God (Phil. ii. 6). How then was this pre-existent Being to be thought of so as not to endanger monotheism? We shall see presently that Paul himself supplied the answer to the question, when he further identified the pre-existent Son of God with the Cosmic Wisdom. It will be seen that the later doctrine of the Trinity has been able to make great and profitable use of this identification.

The risk in the Christology was more serious than the danger to monotheism, as the history of Christian doctrine shows. The result of Phil. ii. 5–11 was that in the general mind of the Church the human life of Jesus became a temporary brief incident in the endlessness backwards and forwards of an Eternal Being.

In this case Paul the Apostle did not himself supply the correction. We have seen what short work he makes of the human life of Jesus, in spite of the centre at once of his preaching and his personal faith being the Cross. The Apostle's apparent lack of interest in the story of Jesus is one of the most puzzling things in the early history of Christianity. He does occasionally refer to the teaching of Jesus, and it is generally recognized that the Pauline ethic is the ethic of Jesus applied to new situations. It has been well said that I Cor. xiii might stand for a character sketch of Jesus. And what is not so often noticed, is that the doctrine of the Spirit in the Pauline Epistles reproduces the exact main features of the religious teaching of Jesus. Jesus called God Father (Abba): the Spirit repeats the name. Jesus demanded righteousness:

the Spirit promotes righteousness. Jesus proclaimed the present and future Kingdom of God: the Spirit is not only the spirit of present sonship and present righteousness, but is also an earnest of immortality.

All this is true: Jesus never had a more devoted disciple than Paul. And yet the enigma remains: why did the Apostle pay so little attention to His life and work in Palestine? We may say that his bent was theological rather than historical. Not for nothing had he sat at the feet of Gamaliel. Not for nothing had he lived in the university city of Tarsus. We may point to the special circumstances of his conversion through the vision of the Risen Christ on the Damascus road, which made him an apostle without serving the apprenticeship Peter and the rest had served in Palestine (Gal. i. 15, 16). But when all is said, we are still left with the problem of so ardent a missionary of Jesus Christ with so little evidence of interest in His historical life, of which he must certainly have known a great deal. It is as puzzling as the strange words in II Cor. v. 16, 'Even though we have known Christ after the flesh, yet now we know Him so no more.'

5. THE SYNOPTIC GOSPELS

Paul's theology is very great and wonderful theology: it is a primary source of nearly all later Christian theology. But as we have seen, there is something lacking to it. That something is the gospel story of Jesus. Here is the necessary corrective of the unbalance of the Pauline Christology which we do not find in Paul himself. The difficulty about the Apostle's apparent disregard of the gospel-story would be mitigated, if we could suppose that his missionary preaching was supplemented by a cate-chetical instruction such as Luke speaks of (Lk. i. 4). It is interesting to note that both Mark and Luke, the authors of two of our gospels, were companions of Paul and could have worked in this way. But it must be admitted that there is nothing to suggest this in the Pauline Epistles.

All the same, we know that Mark did write a gospel some time before A.D. 70, which is considered to have been intended for Rome, and therefore can be regarded as a necessary supplement to the Epistle to the Romans. Ancient tradition makes this gospel a record of the preaching of Peter; the recent form-critics regard it as gathered from the general missionary preaching of the Church. As it stands, it is most clearly an expansion of the original *kerygma*, as has been mentioned before in dealing with Acts x. 36–43. It tells the life-story of Jesus from His baptism by John to His Crucifixion and Resurrection. Jesus is plainly in Mark the man of the *kerygma*, 'anointed' with the Spirit at His baptism, preaching and teaching with charismatic authority as a prophet and not dependent on scribal tradition. He goes about doing good, healing demoniacs and others. His gospel is the advent of the Kingdom of God and His demand repentance. However fragmentary the material from which the Gospel of Mark was put together, the picture of Jesus in its agreement with the independent evidence of Q is convincing. The form-critics have proved no doubt that the sayings, parables, narratives, and miracle-stories are related in the contemporary forms of popular literature; but the figure of Jesus emerges from the whole with overpowering force. As was said when treating of Q, the world has recognized the originality of Jesus. John of Damascus was right when he spoke of His advent as 'the newest of all that was new', effectively disproving the pessimism of Eccles. i. 9, 'there's nothing new under the sun' (*De fid. orth*, III, 1).

In all that has been recounted the Jesus of Mark remains human. Even though the Gospel ends with His resurrection, Jesus Himself ascribes resurrection to the power of God (xii. 24). The essential message of Mark's Gospel is the same as that of the *kerygma*. Jesus of Nazareth, a man approved of God by mighty works and wonders and signs, the Jesus who was crucified, is the Messiah, the Christ. The great moment in the Gospel is when Peter acknowledges this (Mk. viii. 29). And the key-idea of the whole gospel is the gradual disclosure of the Messianic secret. The demons recognize from the first what Jesus is (Mk. i. 24, 34, v. 7); Peter is led to his great confession; finally, Jesus Himself declares His Messiahship before the High Priest (Mk. xiv. 61, 62).

If we ask how Jesus Himself conceived the Messianic office, Mk. xiv. 62 makes it plain that He connected it with the Son of Man of Daniel and Enoch, though only with a forward reference: there is no hint of pre-existence. Consistently with this, we find Him constantly speaking of Himself by that name. Apparently the name was not understood in a Messianic sense at the time either by the people or at first by the disciples. It could mean just 'man' (Ps. viii. 4): the meaning was ambiguous and remained for a time obscure. But to continue—Mark gives us more light on how Jesus Himself thought about the Messianic office. It is clear that the voice at the Baptism represents His inward call to it from God: He takes up the Messiahship as at once God's beloved Son and His Spirit-endowed Servant (Mk. i. 11; Ps. ii. 7; Isa. xlii. 1). We have seen already how Q dwells on the unique filial consciousness which characterized the relation of Jesus to God, and the picture of Mark fully accords (Mk. ix. 7, xii. 6, xiv. 36). But Mk. i. 11 shows us Jesus understanding Messiahship not only as unique Sonship, but also as service. Increasingly in Mark that service is associated not only with Isa. xlii. 1, but also with Isa. liii. (esp. Mk. ix. 12, x. 45). This explains the reference to the Servant in the original *kerygma*, and justifies its development into the form presented by Paul in I Cor. xv. 3. It was natural enough that the original *kergyma* should concentrate on Christ's heavenly Lordship and see forgiveness as His royal gift. But as time went on, memory went back to what Jesus had both done and said. Q and Mark equally stand in proof of this.

There can be no doubt that Mark's story of Jesus is substantially historical. The church of Palestine and elsewhere may have shaped the narratives, but it did not invent them. Nor is it possible to take Messiahship out of the story, as Wrede wanted to do. Jesus was crucified under Pontius Pilate: the Roman historian Tacitus confirms that, and the only explanation of the event is that a Jewish 'Messiah' was regarded as a danger to the State. Jesus Himself only propounded a difficulty about the Davidic descent of the Messiah (Mk. xii. 37); but the people hailed him as the Davidic Messiah (Mk. xi. 10), and that was enough to make a Roman governor anxious. Whatever scruples Pilate had, Jesus was crucified as 'King of the Jews' (Mk. xiv. 26).

The final evidence for the historicity of Mark is in its agreement with the independent testimony of Q: they describe the same Person in different ways. And the Person so described can be understood as the subject of the *kerygma* and of the Pauline gospel, but these in themselves could not have created the figure of Jesus in Q and Mark: here memory speaks, and not faith creating an ideal in which to embody itself. It may perhaps be asked, what all this has to do with the doctrine of the Trinity? The answer is simple: it was the Christology of the primitive church, reacting on the doctrines of God and the Spirit, that necessitated a doctrine of the Trinity. But it is in the historical figure of Jesus that the New Testament Christology touches earth and becomes real. Without that contact, all Christology and the ensuing doctrine of the Trinity would be simply speculation.

But it may be said: the *kerygma* had not one term, but

two, Jesus and the Resurrection (cp. Acts xvii. 18). Is the resurrection of Jesus part of the history? Here the answer is that the resurrection appearances are undoubtedly historical: they set Christianity in motion. How we explain them to ourselves in the twentieth century is another matter: no satisfactory theory, orthodox or unorthodox, holds the field. But the recognition of their veridical character depends on two things, on our regard for what has come out of them in the history of the Church, and still more on the impression made upon us by Jesus and the recognition of His eternal value (cp. Heb. xiii. 8). How we think of the continued existence of Jesus depends on our conception of the relation between eternity and time, a matter which will be discussed later in dealing with the final statement of the doctrines of the Incarnation and the Trinity. But it may be pointed out even at this stage that in Peter's first speech as recorded in Acts ii the Apostle supports the evidence of his senses (ii. 32) by an appeal to metaphysical necessity (ii. 24): it was impossible that it should have been otherwise than as he testifies. The lesson is that we cannot take any phenomenon by itself: it has its ultimate meaning in connection with our total view of the universe.

There is one last question to be asked before we leave Mark. It has been said that Jesus as remembered and depicted in Q and Mark is undoubtedly a man, and that He speaks of Himself without a hint of pre-existence. But does Mark writing for Rome set the well remembered story in a framework of the Hellenistic Christology which begins with the pre-existent Son of God? In Mk. i. 1 we read: 'The beginning of the gospel of Jesus Christ, the Son of God' (though some MSS. omit 'Son of God'). Then in iii. 11 and iv. 7 the demoniacs hail Jesus as Son of God. And finally in Mk. xv. 39 the Centurion at the Cross says: 'Truly, this man was a Son of God' (R.V. marg.). Starting from the last passage and interpreting

D

it to mean that the Centurion took Jesus to be a 'Divine man', a wonder-worker descended from heaven, it is said that Mark intends this to be the impression left on the minds of his readers, and the previous references to the Son of God are to be understood accordingly. Therefore recently the Marcan gospel, in which miracles are so predominant, has been described as an Epiphany: the word ἐπιφάνεια is used in pagan Greek of the appearance of a deity to a worshipper: in II Mac. iii. 24 and xii. 22 it is used of a manifestation of the God of Israel. Mark's 'Epiphany', however, is very different from either the pagan or the Jewish Epiphany: it is focussed at the Cross, it is at the Cross that the centurion acclaims Jesus as a Son of God. The Evangelist is one with the Apostle in preaching Christ crucified, though he does it in a very different way. To sum up, since the gospel of Mark was for Rome and belongs to Hellenistic Christology, it is to be expected that he would write in harmony with Paul's Hellenistic Christology. All the more remarkable is it that the story he tells should be so true to Palestine: the memory of Jesus as He was still triumphed over any tendency to represent Him differently.

The Gospels of Matthew and Luke, written in the last quarter of the first century A.D., combine Mark and Q in different ways. By incorporating the teaching matter of Q in the Marcan story they give us a balanced picture of the personality of Jesus which is of great value. There is some modification of the sources here and there in the interest of the growing Christology of the Church; but essentially Matthew and Luke are still true to Palestine, and hence are called with Mark the three 'Synoptic' Gospels, since they see Jesus from the same point of view.

They unite, however, in going beyond, not only Mark, but also Paul, by adding to the story of Jesus an account of His Virgin birth, though quite differently and irreconcilably as regards detail. The Virgin Birth stands as an explanation of the Divine nature of Jesus, but there is no need to go into the questions arising out of the narratives in a book on the Trinity, as that doctrine depends not on the Virgin Birth of Jesus but on the Pauline Christology of pre-existence.

Another thing that Matthew and Luke add to Mark is the genealogies, both of which go back to David, and then one to Abraham, the other to Adam. Their interest for us is that both illustrate the original *kerygma* of Jesus as the Messiah of Israel (Acts ii. 30, iii. 13), while the genealogy of Luke further illustrates the Pauline transformation of the *kerygma* into the gospel of the Second Adam. It may be added that the genealogies both trace the descent of Jesus through Joseph, who, as Luke says, was his reputed father. They too, like the stories of the Virgin Birth, are in detail irreconcilable. But all these things show how the mind of the Church in the first century was occupied with everything that served to illuminate the *kerygma*.

Finally, Matthew and Luke, each in his own way, add to what they take from Mark and Q, elements from other sources, and expand the story of the life and teaching, sometimes by what is most valuable historically, such as the parable of the Prodigal Son (Lk. xv. 11f.); sometimes, as in the Baptismal formula (Mt. xxviii. 19), by what is clearly due to doctrinal development in the Church. Baptism was originally in the name of Christ only (Acts ii. 38).

6. I PETER AND HEBREWS

The Epistles of Paul and the Synoptic Gospels exhibit complementary developments from the original *kerygma*, the one more doctrinal, the other more historical. There are two epistles in the New Testament where doctrine is more balanced by history than it is in Paul. These are I Peter and the Epistle to the Hebrews. The date and authorship of the beautiful First Epistle of Peter are disputed. 'Hebrews' is certainly not Pauline: the author is unknown, but it dates from the latter part of the first century.

Both epistles have behind them the *kerygma* in the form in which it includes Christ's death for our sins (I Pet. ii. 24; Heb. x. 12). He was foretold and prepared for in prophecy (I Pet. i. 10; Heb. i. 1). He is now the risen and exalted Lord (I Pet. i. 3; Heb. xiii. 20).

But both epistles go beyond the *kerygma*, just as Paul does. In I Peter Christ is thought of as pre-existent; though i. 20 speaks only of God's foreknowledge of Him before the foundation of the world and His subsequent manifestation, yet i. 11 describes the Spirit of Christ as operative in the prophets, just as Paul wrote of Christ as the spiritual rock whence the fathers drank in the desert (I Cor. x. 4).

'Hebrews' has a great Christology which combines Christ's Messianic pre-eminence with a cosmological doctrine resembling that of Paul in Colossians. In Heb. i. 1–4 Christ is described as the Son of God, through whom the worlds were made, and who upholds all things by the word of His power. He has been appointed by God heir of all things. He is the effulgence (ἀπαύγασμα) of God's glory, and the representation (χαρακτήρ) of His substance (ὑπόστασις). As in the case of Paul the parallel with Proverbs and the Wisdom of Solomon and the general agreement with Philo's Logos doctrine are both of them clear. A direct relation to Wisd. vii. 26 is marked by the use of the word ἀπαύγασμα. The word ὑπόστασις, destined to have a great place in the doctrine of the Trinity, is used in Heb. i. 3 for the first time in Christian literature.

There is evidence that it was still necessary to distinguish

Christ from the angels (i. 4f.). He is the firstborn
of creation and superior to the angels, who are God's
ministering spirits. He is by God's command the object
of their worship. His Messianic Kingdom is without end
(cp. xiii. 8). There is the same distinction of Him from
God as in the Pauline epistles. God is His God, who has
anointed Him; that is, has instituted Him as Messiah.
Yet words from Ps. cii. 25f., originally applied to JAHWEH,
are used to prove His eternity. The net result is as in
Phil. ii. 10, 11 and still further back in Acts ii. 21 (taken
with iv. 12), that we have the application to the Lord
Christ of references to the Lord JAHWEH in the Old Testament because Christ is the Representative of God; and
yet the use of the same name 'Lord' in both cases carries
a suggestion of identity between Christ and God which
was bound to be realized by and by.

Where I Peter and Hebrews differ from Paul is in the
interest both of them show in the human experience of
Jesus. While Phil. ii. 5f. is an exhortation to humility
taken from the self-emptying of Christ in the Incarnation,
I Pet. ii. 21–23 dwells at length on Christ's human patience
in His passion and takes an example from that. Hebrews
goes still further. The Epistle refers not only to Christ's
endurance of suffering (xii. 2, 3, xiii. 12), but also to His
experience of temptation (ii. 18, iv. 15), His prayers and
His piety (εὐλάβεια, v. 7). Though He was a Son, He
learned obedience from the things that He suffered (v. 8).
He was made perfect through suffering (ii. 10). He came
to do the will of God (x. 9). He is the leader and perfecter
of faith and an example of endurance (xii. 2). As in the
Synoptic Gospels Jesus is represented as led by the
Spirit (cp. Mk. i. 12 with Heb. ix. 14).

As to the Incarnation, I Pet. i. 20 speaks simply of
Christ's manifestation; but Heb. ii. 14, 17 says that He
partook of flesh and blood, and was made in all things like
His brethren. No more than in the Pauline epistles is

there any explanation of how an Incarnation was possible.

So far I Peter and Hebrews have been considered together, but we now must come to a remarkable peculiarity of Hebrews, which it shares to some extent with the Gospel and First Epistle of John, but with little else in the New Testament. Contemporary Jewish theology distinguished between the present age and the age to come, which would be that of the Messiah and the Kingdom of God. It is a common doctrine in the New Testament that with the coming of Christ into the world the Messianic age is already begun. We have noted the evidence for this teaching in Q and the Pauline Epistles: Hebrews implies the same view in vi. 4, 5. But while the writer does not abandon the primitive expectation of the speedy end of all things (x. 25), he reinterprets the dynamic tension between present and future by means of a static metaphysical distinction between the eternal world, which is real and immutable, and the present mutable and shadowy order, where only copies of things eternal exist (viii. 2, 5, x. 1, xii. 22f.). By means of this distinction Hebrews in quite a different way from that of Paul shows that Christians are independent of the Jewish law: the independence proclaimed in Hebrews is not, however, freedom from a law of works, but freedom from the Jewish ceremonial system. That belongs with its priests and sacrifices to the mutable order of copies and shadows; Christ, though offering a sacrifice on earth (xiii. 12) offers it through the Eternal Spirit (ix. 14), and presents it in heaven, where He not only sits enthroned as Messianic King (i. 3), but also is our High Priest and Intercessor (viii. 1, ix. 24).

There is a mention of the distinction between things temporal and things eternal in II Cor. iv. 18; and in Col. iii. 3 it is said that the life of Christians is even now hid with Christ in God, i.e. belongs to the heavenly and invisible world. But Hebrews carries out the distinction

in a thoroughgoing way, imparting into the whole interpretation of Christianity the principles of the Platonic-
Alexandrian philosophy, of which Philo also is an exponent.
It is interesting to note that Philo also calls the Logos
the High Priest and makes him an intercessor, though of
course without any idea of Incarnation.

The great importance of the Epistle to the Hebrews lies
in the fact that it represents a recognition already awaken-
ing in the early Church, that Christianity implies a
metaphysic, while nevertheless its central theme is of
One who was truly man. As was said before, Dr. Cullmann's
statement that there is no Hellenism in Hebrews or the
Johannine writings can only be regarded as purely
arbitrary. It is of course necessitated by his thesis that
Christianity is committed by the New Testament to the
interpretation of eternity as endlessness, and has nothing
in common with the view of eternity as transcending
time, which is Greek, pagan and anti-Christian.

7. THE JOHANNINE WRITINGS

Only one other New Testament doctrine of primary
importance remains to be studied. We come to the Gospel
and the accompanying First Epistle of John. Both date
from the last years of the first century A.D., and are
probably the work of the same 'John', whoever he was.
It is now very widely recognized that the Gospel is a
work of unique character. It uses history with sovereign
freedom as the vehicle of theological ideas. It resembles
Mark in being the story of the Epiphany of the Son of
God; but, whereas Mark tells the actual story of the
historical Jesus as an Epiphany, John rewrites the history
in terms of a Logos Christology. A prologue states the
doctrine of the Logos and leads up to the moment of the
Incarnation. The gospel story is then retold from the
Baptism to the crucifixion and resurrection, but it is

told as the story of the Incarnate Logos, who has descended from heaven and will return thither. His miracles are signs that manifest His glory (Jn. ii. 11), while in His discourses He reveals what He is, and why He has come. Except only in iii. 5, He speaks, not of the Kingdom of God as in the Synoptic Gospels, but of Himself, in speeches which contain the essence of the Johannine doctrine. It is noteworthy that whether it is John the Baptist, Jesus or the Evangelist himself who speaks, all is in one style and one key; all in fact expound the same doctrine in the same way.

The Fourth Gospel reflects controversies both with the disciples of John the Baptist and with contemporary Judaism, but still more with a Gnosticism of a more advanced type than that attacked in 'Colossians'. This Gnosticism also forms the background of the Epistle. Two features are specially prominent in it. One is the denial of a real Incarnation, which is impossible since the spiritual and the material cannot be united. The other is a libertinism which takes the place of the Colossian ascetism. Since spirit and matter have nothing in common, it can be argued that nothing done in the body can affect the spirit. The Epistle opposes both those heresies in the most outspoken way (I Jn. i. 5, 6, iv. 3). In the Gospel the attack on them is indirect. It opposes to the false Gnosis the true Gnosis, which Jesus has brought (Jn. xvii. 3), together with the accompanying ethical demand (Jn. xv. 12).

In the Prologue to the Gospel the great word, Logos, which is not in the Pauline Epistles or in Hebrews, is at last spoken; thus their meaning finds its final and perfect expression. But it is noteworthy that John distinguishes, as they do not, between the Son and the hypostasis with which He is identified. The Logos is spoken of personally in Jn. i. 1 only in the way that a hypostasis is personalized in Prov. viii. 22, 30. This is made perfectly plain when we

compare I Jn. i. 2, where in impersonal terminology the
Incarnation is spoken of as the manifestation of the
eternal life which was with the Father from the beginning.
This is, however, only one evidence that the personal
language of Jn. i. 1 can not be pressed. Another is the
remarkable parallel with Wisd. viii. 3, where Wisdom
(in ix. 1 equated with Word) is said to live with God and
be loved by God, and in ix. 4 to sit by Him on His throne.
Finally, the text Jn. i. 1 itself is sufficient evidence when
read in the original, which may be translated: 'In the
beginning was the Logos, and the Logos was with God,
and the Logos was Divine.' The above translation accurately reproduces the distinction between ὁ Θεός (with the
article), which means 'God', and Θεός (without the article),
which means 'Divine'. The Logos, then, is only personalized as a hypostasis; and the fully personal name
'Son' is reserved for Jesus, the result of the Incarnation
(Jn. i. 14–18). We note further that when in the body of
the Gospel Jesus is made to speak of descending from
heaven (vi. 38), or of His glory with the Father before the
world was (xvii. 5), these things are said from the standpoint of the Incarnate Son, who in thought carries back
His present personal form of existence into eternity.
It is a different point of view from that of the Prologue.

To continue, then, with what the Prologue says: All
things were made by the Logos, which is the life and light
of men. Incarnate in Jesus Christ, God's unique Son
(μονογενής), who is in the closest communion with the
Father, He has revealed God, whose transcendence is
strongly emphasized (Jn. i. 3–18). The body of the Gospel
is the story of the revelation.

It is important to observe that for all his advanced
Christology John develops his doctrine from the primitive *kerygma*. Jesus is the Spirit-endowed Messiah foretold
in prophecy (Jn. i. 32, 45, iv. 25, 26), who died for our
sins (Jn. i. 29; I Jn. i. 7), and rose again from the dead

(Jn. xx. 1f.). His second coming is expected (I Jn. ii. 28), as Judge of men (Jn. v. 28, 29). But all is reinterpreted. There is no gradual disclosure of the Messianic secret. Jesus is known as Messiah from the first. More than that, the judgment is now (Jn. iii. 18, v. 24, 28). It takes place in the separation between belief and unbelief. Jesus Himself is the Resurrection and the Life (xi. 25). He is glorified already in His death (xii. 25f.). All is spiritualized and translated out of the language of time into that of eternity. Eternal life is now (v. 24), given in the knowledge of God and of Jesus Christ (xvii. 3). The Messianic Kingdom of Jesus becomes the kingdom of the truth (xviii. 36, 37). As in the Epistle to the Hebrews, we have a doctrine of salvation that transcends time: as in that Epistle, the true is the real; we move in the atmosphere of the contemporary Platonism. True and Truth occur constantly in a Platonic sense in the Fourth Gospel. The meaning comes out clearly in vi. 32 where Jesus as the true bread from heaven which gives eternal life is opposed to the manna which was temporal and perishing, and had no such result; cp. also I Jn. v. 20.

Though John retains from the *kerygma* the doctrine of the sacrifice for sin, and thus maintains it in the form stated by Paul (I Cor. xv. 3), nevertheless this is not with the intention of making the Cross the centre of the gospel in the Pauline way. On the contrary, with John redemption by the death of Christ (Jn. i. 29; I Jn. i. 7, ii. 2) is absorbed in the wider setting of revelation. The Logos is the life and light of men (Jn. i. 4), and the story of Jesus, the Incarnate Logos, is told so as to show how He brings both. His whole earthly life is a revelation of God, and faith is one with knowledge.

What then is the relation of Jesus Christ to the transcendent God whom He reveals (Jn. i. 18)? They are the Father and the Son. In the Fourth Gospel the name Father is used for God almost exclusively with reference to Jesus; whereas in the Synoptics God is mostly spoken of as the Father of men in general, and in the Pauline Epistles there is a balance between the two significances. The unity of the Father and the Son is a constant theme in the Johannine speeches of Jesus. The Father has given all things into His hand (Jn. iii. 35). In all that He does He is one with the Father and has equal honour with Him (v. 17, 19, 23). Jesus says 'I and the Father are one', and again, 'The Father is in me and I in the Father' (x. 30, 38). According to the context 'one' (Gk. ἕν, which is neuter) stands here primarily for moral unity, but it carries with it a further suggestion of unity of nature or being; for John introduces a Jewish accusation that Jesus blasphemes (x. 36), or that Jesus has made Himself equal with God (v. 18). In this connection we may recall the further words of Jesus in viii. 58, 'Before Abraham was I am', remembering that 'I AM' is the name of God in Ex. iii. 14.

It is, however, remarkable that Jesus meets the Jewish accusation by appealing to Ps. lxxxii. 6, where those who represent God are called gods (Jn. x. 34–36). There is here the same minimizing of the full idea of Deity with regard to the Incarnate Logos that we noted before with respect to the pre-existent Logos in i. 1. In fact, Jesus emphasizes His continual dependence on the Father in v. 19, 30; and He says not only, 'The Father is greater than all' (x. 29), but also, in so many words, 'The Father is greater than I' (xiv. 28). Finally, while Thomas calls the Risen Christ 'My Lord and my God' (xx. 28), the Risen Christ Himself bids Mary Magdalene tell the brethren, 'I ascend unto my Father and your Father, and my God and your God' (xx. 17).

The Gospel of John has not only a great Christology, but also the most advanced Pneumatology to be found in the New Testament. As with Paul the Spirit is the principle of regeneration (iii. 5). But the teaching goes far beyond this. In the farewell discourses, xiv–xvi, Jesus tells the disciples that when He leaves this world, His place will be supplied by another Paraclete or Helper, who is the Spirit of Truth (xiv. 16, 17). The Spirit proceeds from the Father (xv. 26); and it is said that Jesus will send Him, or otherwise that the Father will send Him in Christ's name (xiv. 26, xv. 26). Moreover, the coming of the Spirit is identified with the second coming of Christ. There is an unmistakeable interchange between the two in xiv. 16–18, 26–28; and the transformation of Christ's eschatological coming into His presence in the Spirit is further marked by the repeated use of the Old Testament eschatological phrase 'in that day' (Isa. ii. 12–20, iv. 2, xii. 1) to describe the age of the Spirit (Jn. xiv. 20, xvi. 23, 26). The interchange between Jesus and the Spirit shows moreover that the Spirit is conceived in the farewell discourse as a Personal Being like Jesus Himself.

It remains to say a word about the Johannine doctrine of God. The stress on the Divine transcendence (Jn. i. 18) has been noted already, also the almost total restriction of the name Father to God's relation to Jesus. But no account of John's doctrine of God can be complete without a mention of the three great sayings: 'God is Spirit' (iv. 24); 'God is Light' (I Jn. i. 5); 'God is Love' (I Jn. iv. 8). In their apparent simplicity they furnish an inexhaustible material for a definitive doctrine of God.

Like the Epistles of Paul, the Gospel and Epistle of John well illustrate what has been called the ambivalence or two-way character of the developed New Testament doctrine. There is a Rabbinic element in the discourses of Jesus. There seems, moreover, to be an Aramaic origin for some of the matter which the Gospel contains. It is no wonder therefore that some scholars should be impressed with its relation to the Old Testament and Rabbinic Judaism, and that the hypostatized Logos or Word in Jn. i. 1 should be explained by them through

reference to Isa. lv. 11, Ps. xxx. 6 and cxlvii. 15, 18, 19,
along with the Wisdom figure and Rabbinic ideas about
the pre-existence of the Torah (the Mosaic law). Others
are impressed by the general parallelism with Philo in
his use of the term Logos with all its philosophical connotation. More recently parallels have been drawn with
the Hermetic literature, which also blended Greek
philosophy with Judaism. Most recently of all has the
Gnostic background been emphasized which has been
described already. The true explanation of the Johannine
literature is that it is a review of the gospel in the light
of the general higher religion of the first century, so as to
present it in a way that would make it at once intelligible
and convincing to those with such a preparation. The
constant antitheses, Light and Darkness, Truth and the
Lie, Above and Below, Heavenly and Earthly, Freedom
and Bondage, all belong to the Gnostic vocabulary with
its sharp distinction of the spiritual and the material;
but John gives them not only a metaphysical but also an
ethical reference, which appears especially in the Epistle
passim, but also characterizes the Gospel. But the great
key-word of the Gospel is another word of the higher
non-Christian religion: it is Logos. The very essence of
both Gospel and Epistle is the identification of the Logos
with the historical Jesus Christ. For this purpose John
retells the gospel story so as to mark both the Divinity
and the humanity of Jesus. It must be admitted that in
spite of references to His human experience (e.g. Jn. iv.
6, xi. 33, 35, xiii. 22) the predominant picture is that of
Divine omniscience and omnipotence in human form
(e.g. Jn. i. 48, 50, ii. 24, 25, iii. 52, 53, xii. 30, xviii. 6).
The theology in short predominates over the history: a
perfect balance and union of the two is not achieved.
Nevertheless, the Gospel of John is the last word in New
Testament theology. It says once for all what Paul did
not say, that the Gospel must be exhibited in the whole

historical life of Jesus Christ. If John has too much revised the Synoptic story in the endeavour to show its Divine meaning, we still have the Synoptic Gospels by which to check his work. The final aim of Christian theology must be to carry out the Johannine conception of the Divinity of the Gospel story without losing the human Jesus of the Synoptics. In the Synoptic Gospels the theological setting has not overpowered the history.

8. THE UNITY OF THE NEW TESTAMENT

We have now studied all the New Testament writings really important for the doctrine of the Trinity. There remain a few other books, the Apocalypse, the Pastoral Epistles and the great bulk of the Catholic Epistles, only I Peter and I John having been discussed among the latter. Out of the above list, II and III John go with I John, but add nothing for our purpose. The rest of the books like the Johannine literature appear to belong to the later age of primitive Christianity, not differing very greatly in character from the 'Apostolic Fathers' of the second century A.D.: in fact the Church in fixing the Canon of the New Testament had considerable trouble in drawing the line between the two groups. However, the books we are speaking of were included finally in the New Testament, and something therefore must be said of them, especially in view of the recent emphasis on the unity of the New Testament.

In general these writings are not concerned with doctrine, but with eschatology, ethics and church-order. But of course doctrine is implied, and we note the common agreement with the major books already considered. There is the same emphasis on Monotheism (Jas. ii. 19; I Tim. i. 17, ii. 5; cp. Rev. xxii. 8, 9). There is a remarkable description of the Divine transcendence in I Tim. vi. 15,

16; cp. also i. 17. There is next the same double attitude to Jesus Christ.

On the one hand He is associated with God (Rev. xi. 15, xii. 10), He is 'King of Kings and Lord of Lords' (Rev. xvii. 14, xix. 16). He is the First and the Last (Rev. i. 17), and is described in terms that recall the Ancient of Days in Dan. vii. 9, 13, who is the God of Israel (Rev. i. 14). His kingdom is eternal (II Pet. i. 11). If God is our Saviour (I Tim. iv. 10), so is He: He is so called frequently in the Pastoral Epistles, II Peter and Jude. 'Soter' (Saviour) is one of the two-way religious words of the time: it belongs to the Old Testament (Isa. xlv. 21, LXX), and is also in constant use in Hellenistic religion for the special protective Divinity, or for the 'Divine man'. It is also found in the *kerygma* of Acts v. 31, and appears in Phil. iii. 20, Lk. ii. 11, Jn. iv. 42. But it is found no less than six times in Titus, and five in II Peter. Whether Christ is actually called God in Tit. ii. 13 is matter of dispute: see the R.V. margin. But in Rev. xix. 13 He is called the Logos, as in Jn. i. 1.

On the other hand, the humanity of Jesus is emphasized. He is man (I Tim. ii. 5), of the seed of David (II Tim. ii. 8; Rev. xxii. 16). He witnessed the good confession before Pilate (I Tim. vi. 13). A description of His saving work which is interesting as linking the fringe of the New Testament with the Apostolic Fathers is found in II Tim. i. 10: He has 'abolished death' and has 'brought life and incorruption to light through the gospel'.

The Holy Spirit is spoken of as regenerative (Tit. iii. 16). He spoke in the prophets (II Pet. i. 21), and still speaks in the prophecy of the Church (Rev. xix. 10). A curious feature in the Book of Revelation is the mention of seven spirits of God (i. 4, iii. 1, iv. 5, v. 6). It is worth while recording, because it shows how fluid was the conception of the spirit. The seven spirits are probably the same as the seven angels of viii. 2, since the description of their function is the same in both cases: they are again to be identified with the seven Archangels of Judaism (cp. Tobit xii. 15).

We are come to the end of our long study of the New Testament writers. Mention has been made of the recent stress on the unity of the New Testament. A unity there is, but it is one of attitude, not of doctrine. There is the same attitude to Jesus Christ as Lord and Saviour expressed in ever developing forms of doctrine from the *kerygma* onwards. The doctrine in all its forms is charismatic, i.e. it is of the nature of prophecy, proceeding from the inspiration of the Spirit (Acts ii. 4, 17, 18, v. 32, vi. 10; I Cor. ii. 10, xii. 8; II Cor. iii. 6; Jn. xiv. 26; I Jn. iv. 4; Rev. ii. 7). But that does not mean that there are no human factors. The gracious warmth of the Spirit kindles the human elements into a flame, so that they combine in new forms, altogether unprecedented. The three human factors of doctrine are always Authority, Reason and Experience. For the New Testament writers Authority meant the Old Testament; Reason was formally argument, materially the current thought of the religious and philosophical environment. These two factors we have had continually before us; but little has been said about the third factor of Experience, except in so far as there has been mention of the forgiveness of sins and the regenerating power of the Spirit, which are not just doctrines or even simply Divine promises (Acts ii. 38, 39), but also are verified in peace with God (Rom. v. 1), joy (Rom. xiv. 17), patience and hope (Rom. v. 3, 4), and moral freedom (Rom. viii. 4f.) which works out in the love described in I Cor. xiii. All these references are taken from Paul, but they can be paralleled from other New Testament writers in abundance. The sum and substance of all is that the New Testament contains the record of an experience, whose gracious character shines out all the more clearly the more it is set over against the prevailing despondency of the age. The Jew says: 'My heart failed me' (IV Ezra iii. 29): the Pagan did not know whether to blame *Tyche* (Chance) or *Heimarmene* (Fate) for his misfortunes. [See Wendland, *Die Hellenistische-Romische Kultur*, pp. 59–61.] It was the experience of forgiveness and new freedom that characterized the primitive church in the first century; and it was this experience combining with authority and reason in Apostolic minds that brought about the prophecy which we call New Testament doctrine, the whole being fused by the fire of the spirit and crystallizing in the forms which we have been studying.

If we ask what was the origin of the whole, the Spirit-endowed Church, its experience and its doctrine, the answer is plain, it was Jesus. He it was from whom came the whole 'new creation' (II Cor. v. 17). Consequently, it was as Christology that the crystallization of New Testament doctrine began, when in so many different ways Apostles and Evangelists strove to say what they had found in Jesus. For all He was the Lord and Christ of the original *kerygma*; but prophetic doctrine went on to transform the *kerygma* into a universal gospel, and in the process the Old Testament conceptions of God and the Spirit were also transformed, with the result that the New Testament as we have it became the matrix of the doctrine of the Trinity, as has been said before.

II.—THE PATRISTIC DEVELOPMENT

1. THE BEGINNINGS

FROM the first anticipations of the doctrine of the Trinity in the New Testament we go on to its definitive formation in the patristic period. Authority, reason and experience still continue to be the factors of doctrinal development, but both their character and their relations suffer change. In the charismatic theology of the New Testament they were fused by the *charisma*. Now as time goes on, the first enthusiasm gives way to a more reflective temper. So far as the *charisma* still continues, now located as we shall see in bishop and council, it is no longer such as to fuse the elements of doctrine anew and create fresh forms, but only such as to weld authority and reason together when they become distinct from one another. As to experience, it is still involved through the control exercised over other doctrines by the conception of salvation, but the control is indirect: the prominent factors of doctrine in the patristic period are authority and reason. Authority grows in quantity from only that of the Old Testament to the larger scope of the authority of the Creed, the Scriptures of both Testaments, and episcopal tradition. Reason stands for the philosophical heritage of Greece, concentrated in the idea of the Logos. As we have seen, this idea was the point where Greek philosophy touched the New Testament. But the charismatic New Testament writings also contained many other points of doctrine, especially those that found formulation in the Creed. Here was the origin of a tension which resulted in doctrinal formation.

It was the crisis created by the upsurge of Gnostic heresy in the second century which led to the establishment of the New Testament as an authoritative standard of doctrine in addition to the Old Testament, which was the Church's authority from the beginning. But, as has just been said, the Creed and episcopal tradition were also authoritative. We have now to consider these in their relation to the New Testament. In order to fix this relation something more must be said about Gnosticism. It was presented in all its varied forms as a higher knowledge (Gnosis), superior to the common belief of Christians and destined to supersede it. Its fundamental principles have been explained during our study of the New Testament. We may recall (1) the dualism of God and matter as an opposition of good and evil, or of light and darkness, and (2) the attempt to fill the gap between Absolute Deity and matter by a number of intermediate spiritual beings: these were conceived in the different Gnostic systems in the most bizarre forms, whether as hypostatized abstractions, angelic powers or minor divinities, with names culled in part from Greek philosophy and in part from the various Oriental religions, including Judaism and Christianity. Gnosticism came into conflict with the faith of the Christian Church on two points above all. One was its break with monotheism—not only did it recognize intermediate spiritual powers, but also in regarding matter as altogether alien from God it controverted the Old Testament doctrine of God as the creator of all things whatsoever. The second point of difference was in the attitude taken up to Jesus Christ. It was the Gnostics who first found a problem in the Person of Christ, where Paul, the author of Hebrews, and John, for all their high Christology, had seen none. The Gnostics accepted from Christianity the belief that Jesus Christ was a Saviour, and they were willing to accord Him a place in their spiritual hierarchy, but their absolute dualism of spirit and matter at once created a difficulty as to the constitution of His Person. We have had occasion already to note that the first century Gnostics denied that Jesus Christ was come in the flesh. The second century Gnostics repeated the denial. They could not conceive of any real union between spirit and matter. So some said that the human form of Jesus was mere appearance; such a view is known as Docetism, a name derived from the Greek word δοκέω meaning, 'I appear'. Others allowed Jesus to be a real man, but regarded the association of the spiritual Christ with the man as accidental and temporary: it began at John's baptism and ended before the crucifixion.

If Gnosticism was a danger to Christianity in the first century, it became much more so in the second century: towards the end of the century the danger became extreme. The charismatic character of primitive Christian doctrine allowed the infiltration of all manner of strange teachings, there being so little definition of what was Christian and what was not. Moreover, the authority of the Old Testament, hitherto fundamental for Christians, was shaken by Gnostic criticism. The Church found leaders in the great Antignostic Fathers, Irenæus, Tertullian and Clement of Alexandria; and the danger was met and overcome. Ramparts were established against Gnostic infiltration. The result is known to historians as the founding of the Ancient Catholic Church, of which Catholicity or universality was one mark, while Apostolicity was the other.

The first bulwark against Gnosticism was set up by the recognition of the baptismal confession as the Rule of Faith. Here it was the confession of the Roman church about A.D. 150 that set the pattern. Its sentences can be recovered from the writings of Justin Martyr, Irenæus and Tertullian: in substance it differed little from what to-day is known as the 'Apostles' Creed. This Creed or

Rule of Faith stood as a concise statement of the common belief of all true Christians.

The second defence against Gnosticism was the tradition of the bishops of the great metropolitan churches, believed to have been founded by the Apostles. This additional defence was necessary, because the Gnostics not only criticized the Old Testament, but also allegorized the gospel story, applying to the common faith of the church the method hitherto used by the Church itself upon the Old Testament. As the Church had extracted Christian teaching from the Old Testament by allegorization, so the Gnostics drew their doctrines out of the Christian history of Jesus and the Apostles by means of a similar process. Moreover, they claimed to have a secret tradition of interpretation from the Apostles themselves: this claim the leaders of the Church denied, saying that the true Christian tradition was located in the bishops who were the manifest successors of the Apostles. The bishops were thus the inheritors of Apostolic truth; but Irenæus goes beyond this and asserts that the bishop as the successor of the Apostles has also inherited a charismatic certainty in regard to the truth. This meant that the charismatic character, formerly belonging to the whole church, was now restricted to the bishop. It explains why later on doctrinal disputes were settled by gathering together councils of bishops.

We are now in a position to see exactly how and where the New Testament came in as an authoritative standard of doctrine. The third and last defence against Gnosticism was built by the maintenance of the authority of the Old Testament and by the addition to it of the books of the New Testament as equally authoritative. The fact that the New Testament Canon was formed not all at once but gradually is here unimportant, as the most essential books doctrinally were included from the first. But the gradualness throws light on the intention of the Canon: it was

formed by a slow sifting of the charismatic writings
available and the selection of what was believed to be
genuinely Apostolic. It was with the help of the creed
and episcopal tradition that the sifting took place. But
when once the New Testament Canon had come into
existence, the Scriptures of both Testaments came to be
the supreme authority, the Creed being regarded as a
compendium of Biblical teaching, and the bishops themselves being judged by their agreement with the Scriptures.

It should be added that what has been said applies
properly to the West, where the Creed was more legally
construed as the Rule of Faith. In the East not only was
there at first less credal precision, but also there was
more direct appeal to the Scriptures.

Such then were the formal conditions for the development of doctrine in the Church, but there were material
conditions also. These are revealed by (1) the contents
of the Creed, (2) the theology of the 'Apostolic Fathers',
and (3) that of the Apologists of the second century.

(I) The Creed is of the greatest importance. There was
variation of the baptismal confession from Church to
Church; but, as has been noted, it was the Roman creed
that set the pattern for doctrine, at any rate in the West.
The main features of the present 'Apostles' Creed' are
visible in Justin Martyr's first *Apology* (c. A.D. 150) and
his *Dialogue with Trypho the Jew* (A.D. 155–160). The
details are given in Hahn's *Bibliothek der Symbole und
Glaubensregeln der Alten Kirche*. We find mentioned
(*a*) God the Father and Master of all things, (*b*) Jesus
Christ, the Son of God our Saviour, born of a virgin,
crucified under Pontius Pilate, risen again and ascended
into heaven and expected to come again as Judge of all
men, and (*c*) the Holy Spirit. The origination of the
credal elements from the baptismal formula in Mt. xxviii.
19 and the *kerygma* is plain.

How and when exactly the Roman baptismal confession

took shape is uncertain. The earliest clear evidence for
it is in Justin, but it is undoubtedly considerably earlier
than his above mentioned works.

(II) We come next to the 'Apostolic Fathers', including
what are known as the Epistles of Clement of Rome,
Polycarp and Barnabas, the 'Shepherd' of Hermas, and
the 'Didache' or 'Teaching of the Twelve Apostles'.
Their date is from A.D. 90 to 140; and they represent the
common Christianity of the period, so far as it is untouched by Gnosticism. As has been said already, they are
akin to the books on the fringe of the New Testament.

The 'Apostolic Fathers' can help us in two ways.
They show, if proof be needed, that the articles of belief
assembled in the Creed were common property in the
Church. The unity of God and His Creatorship is the
prime article of faith for Hermas (*Mand.* i, 1); the
Christological articles of the Creed can all be found in
Ignatius (*Magn.*, xi; *Trall.*, ix; *Smyrn.*, i, etc.; I Clement
(xlvi. 6 and lviii. 2) combines the One God and the One
Christ with the Holy Spirit.

But, if we seek for further interpretations of these
articles of faith, there is not a great deal; only Hermas and
Ignatius really carry us forward. There can be observed,
however, in the Apostolic Fathers a general view of the
Christian religion which is of great importance as providing
the atmosphere in which doctrinal development took
place. The things that are valued are not the elaborate
conceptions and arguments of Paul's soteriology, but
rather the simpler ideas of his natural theology, including
the knowledge of the One God and of His moral law,
together with the promise of immortality (ἀφθαρσία,
literally incorruption) to those who keep the law. But it is
added that all these things are revealed and guaranteed
by Jesus Christ; and this addition transforms the natural
theology into a simplified and moralized version of
Johannine Christianity.

What doctrinal development there is, is found naturally enough in the sphere of Christology: it is here that Hermas and Ignatius make their special contributions. The general background from which they start can, however, be described in two quotations from II Clement, which may stand here for the Christology of the 'Apostolic Fathers' as a whole. They are as follows: (1) 'Brethren, we ought to think of Christ as of God, as of the Judge of the living and the dead' (i.1); (2) 'Christ the Lord, who saved us, being first spirit, became flesh' (ix. 5).

Hermas, sharing the belief expressed in the second quotation, has expanded it into a peculiar Christology of his own. He identifies the pre-existent Christ with the Holy Spirit, whom he calls the 'Son of God'. His doctrine is worked out in his fifth Parable. God made His Spirit, who created the whole creation, to dwell in the flesh which He chose. The flesh was subject to the Spirit, and remained holy and pure. It was therefore rewarded by becoming a partner with the Holy Spirit, and it became an example showing that all flesh in which the Holy Spirit dwells, if it remains undefiled, will receive a reward. Hermas calls the indwelt flesh the 'Servant'. His doctrine obviously has affinities with Rom. i. 1–4 and Phil. ii. 5–11. But he goes altogether beyond them to a definitely adoptianist Christology. The flesh, or the man, by obedience to the Spirit, becomes a partner with Him; or, in other words, becomes 'Son' by adoption.

Hermas is important, not only for Christology, but also for the doctrine of the Trinity. By identifying the pre-existent Christ with the Holy Spirit he sets the pattern for a doctrine of two Persons only in the Godhead instead of three: this doctrine has been called Binitarianism.

Ignatius, to whom we come next, is important because he prefigures the soteriology which was ultimately to determine the patristic Trinitarianism. In this soteriology he transcends the common level of the thought of the

'Apostolic Fathers'. He has certainly no definite construction of the Person of Christ to support his soteriology. He simply recognizes Him as both Divine and human. He was with the Father before the worlds and appeared at the end of time (*Magn.*, vi, 1). After the flesh He was of David's race (Eph. xx. 2), and was subject to the Father (*Magn.*, xiii, 2). Ignatius marks the contrast between the two aspects of His Being. He was Eternal, Invisible, Impalpable, Impassible, and yet He suffered for our sakes (*ad Polyc.*, iii, 2).

Even where Ignatius shares the common view of the 'Apostolic Fathers', he expresses himself in an original way. Christ is the Mind of the Father (Eph. iii. 2), the Word (Logos) in which God breaks His silence (*Magn.*, vi, 2), the unerring Mouth by which the Father has spoken (Rom. viii. 2). From this point of view Christianity is a doctrine of immortality (*Magn.*, vi, 2). Compare Jn. xvii. 3.

But Ignatius adds to this Johannine foundation a Pauline superstructure; it is here that the difference of his soteriology from that of the other Apostolic Fathers manifests itself. Ignatius is influenced by Paul's conception of the Second Adam, and speaks of the dispensation (οἰκονομία) whose end is the new man, Jesus Christ, and which consists in faith and love towards Him in His passion and resurrection (Eph. xx. 1). Christ has brought about the abolition of death (Eph. xix. 3), and has communicated immortality to the Church (Eph. xvii. 1). The gospel is the completion of immortality (*Philad.*, ix, 2).

This is the Pauline Christological soteriology or soteriological Christology, in which the death and resurrection of Christ are inclusive acts, abolishing death and procuring immortality for those who are joined to to Him in faith. What marks Ignatius out from the common level of his age is that he has achieved a combination of theological elements both from Paul and from John, thus anticipating the victorious theology of the future. It is true that he is not a systematic writer: if anyone deserves the description of charismatic, it is he. Only by looking back from the later more definite doctrine of Irenæus can we see how Ignatius had already prepared the way for it. But when our eyes are opened to the fact, there is no doubt that the beginnings, not only of Irenæan, but also of Athanasian theology are to be found in his epistles.

(III) The Apologists of the second century furnish the third material condition of the further development of doctrine. In them we see how already before the founding of the Ancient Catholic Church a powerful philosophical factor was introduced into the statement of Christianity, with the result that the simple second century view of it as the knowledge of God and of His law with the promise of immortality, was transformed into a closely reasoned rational scheme whose centre was the conception of the Logos.

The Apologists we have to deal with are Aristides, Justin, Tatian, Athenagoras and Theophilus (*c.* A.D. 140–180). We have seen that the substance of the Logos-idea is to be found in Paul and Hebrews: the actual term is used by John and is repeated by Ignatius. But it now receives a thorough philosophical treatment. Whereas the New Testament writers had translated the original Messianic *kerygma* into a terminology intelligible to the Hellenistic world, the Apologists made this terminology into the substance of their doctrine, so as to Hellenize Christianity not only in form but also in matter. In the New Testament and by Ignatius the term 'Logos' is used incidentally in stating the Christian message: the Apologists made Christianity an incident of the Logos doctrine. The common belief that Christianity means God, His law and immortality is transformed into the doctrine that Christianity is one with universal Reason, having the same content.

The substance of the doctrine of the Apologists is as follows:

Reason (Logos) is immanent in every man. In the pagan world, however, men had been seduced into idolatry by the demons. Only the finest spirits, such as Socrates and Plato, had followed the instruction of the Logos and had attained the truth. For the great mass of mankind, therefore, a fresh manifestation of the Logos was necessary. It took place through the prophets of the Old Testament, and then in Christ, in Whom the Logos became man. The prophets not only taught the true moral religion, but also, being inspired by the Logos, predicted His incarnation in Jesus. The agreement of the events of His life with the prophetic predictions sets the seal upon the prophetic religion, proving it to be from God and true.

The Apologists made use of rational proofs for the existence of God. They also maintained the authority of the Old Testament, having in allegorization the means of rendering innocuous anything in it that appeared to conflict with rational religion. This attitude of the Apologists to the Old Testament, together with their acceptance of the credal articles, differentiated them from the Gnostics and rendered their philosophizing unobjectionable to the leaders of the Church. The Gnostics had not only criticized the Old Testament, but had also allegorized the gospel story. They did these things because much more than the Apologists they saw in Christianity a religion of redemption 'from this evil world', as Paul had done (Gal. i. 4); their philosophical dualism, however, in which they went beyond Paul, brought them into conflict with the Creed. The Apologists were saved from such conflict by making little attempt to interpret the credal articles, beyond what was implied by the Logos philosophy, their real interest being in the commendation of Christianity to the pagan world as a rational religion. The one place that their scheme allowed for redemption was in the overcoming of the seduction of the demons by a fresh revelation of the truth. Only Justin here furnishes some exception, forming a point of transition betwen Ignatius and Irenæus by introducing into the doctrine of Christ as the head of a new humanity the key-idea of recapitulation (ἀνακεφαλαίωσις), of which Irenæus was to make such powerful use. The corresponding verb ἀνακεφαλαιόομαι appears in the Greek of Eph. i. 10.

The real impact of the Apologists on theology, however, was through their full development of the doctrine of the Logos, to which we now proceed. The starting point is in their emphasis on the Divine transcendence, where they shared the outlook of the eclectic philosophy of their time. This emphasis brought them into conflict with the anthropomorphism of the Old Testament descriptions of God. Certainly the Old Testament itself proclaims the Divine transcendence (Exod. xxxiii. 20; Isa. lv. 8, 9, lvii. 15); but it is not in such a way as to conflict with the primary belief that He is a living God. I Tim. vi. 15, 16 shows that early Christianity followed the Old Testament line. But to minds schooled by Greek philosophy all anthropomorphism could only be figurative; such had been the philosophical expedient in dealing with religion ever since the days of Xenophanes. And so the Apologists teach that God can be truly described only in negative terms—Justin speaks for them all when he calls God 'nameless' (*Dial.*, 127). He is eternal and unbegotten (*Apol.* II, 6), unmoved (*Dial.*, 127).

Hence the necessity of the Logos as a bridge between God and the world. It was through the Logos that He made the world, and it was the Logos that conversed with men, where theophanies are recorded in the Old Testament (Justin, *Dial.*, 128).

What, then, is the Logos? He is identified with the

'Wisdom' of Prov. viii. 22, where the Septuagint reads: 'The Lord created (ἔκτισεν) me as the beginning of His ways towards His works.' Therefore Justin calls the Logos the first offspring (γέννημα) of God (*Dial.*, 62). He is begotten of the Father, as we see one fire originating from another (*Dial.*, 128). His generation is an act of the Father's will (*ib.*). He originates, however, not by a cutting off, as though divided from the Being (οὐσία) of the Father (*ib.*). Tatian speaks to the same effect. Athenagoras explains that the production of the Logos does not mean His coming into existence: 'God had the Logos within Him from the beginning, being eternally rational (λογικός) [*Legatio*, 10]. Theophilus uses the Stoic terminology of the immanent Logos (λόγος ἐνδιάθετος) and the Logos uttered (λόγος προφορικός) in order to differentiate beween the Logos within God and the Logos put forth from God (*Ad Autolycum.*, II, 22).

Justin further says of the Logos that He is a second God, other in number, though not in will (*Dial.*, 56). And so, though other Apologists are more reticent, the word has been spoken, and the Philonic conception of a second God enters patristic theology. The proper comment on such a procedure was made later on by pseudo-Athanasius: 'He who says two Gods, Hellenizes' (*Oratio IV contra Arianos*, 10).

It was remarked before that the Apologists make little attempt to interpret the credal articles beyond what is implied by the Logos philosophy. That means that the interpretation is confined to two points only: (1) God is the Maker of heaven and earth, not directly, but through the Logos; (2) the Son of God of the Creed is the Logos, and the begetting of the Son is the same thing as the production of the Logos. This complete identification of the Son and the Logos is of the greatest importance for the further development of the patristic theology.

The Apologists do little for Pneumatology. All stand

on the baptismal confession, and all regard the Holy Spirit
as pre-existent. Athenagoras calls Him an effluence from
God (*Leg.*, 10), while Theophilus identifying the Spirit
with Wisdom, clearly distinguishes Him from the Logos
(*Ad. Autolycum.*, I, 7, II, 15): in II. 15 he speaks of the
Triad (τριάς), God, His Logos, and His Wisdom. This is
the first definite theological mention of a Trinity.

2. IRENÆUS

The doctrine of the Apologists appeared to the leading
men in the Church to be no more than a translation of the
common Christianity into scientific terminology, and
to be valuable as a defence of Christian teaching addressed
to the higher thought of Paganism. It undermined none
of the historical credal articles, and in this was unlike
Gnosticism. The Fathers who were instrumental in
founding the Ancient Catholic Church had therefore no
difficulty in accepting the Apologetic theology as the
foundation of their own. Irenæus, though not an Apologist,
can use it as a starting-point: this is even more the case
with Tertullian, who was himself an Apologist. Clement
of Alexandria may be said to revise the Apologetic
theology in view of new circumstances.

There were, however, some Christians of the time who
adhered to the Creed, but disliked the philosophy that
had been added to it. Such were the Alogi (Irrationals),
who in their zeal against the Logos doctrine, rejected the
gospel of John. What impelled them was their antagonism
to Montanism, a movement which sought to maintain the
original charismatic character of Christianity, founding
itself on the promise of the Paraclete in Jn. xiv. 16.
Beginning in the second half of the second century,
Montanism came into conflict with the bishops, and was
cut off from the Catholic Church, to which its extreme
rigorism as well as its unrestrained enthusiasm was

altogether objectionable. But the movement made many converts, including the great Antignostic Father Tertullian. He appeals to the Paraclete, i.e. to Montanist prophecy in support of his Trinitarian doctrine: it was their tendency in this direction centering in the idea of the Logos, that provoked the Alogi. It is only through Tertullian, however, that Montanism has left any permanent mark on the formation of doctrine.

But before Tertullian was Irenæus (*d.c.* A.D. 200). He came from Asia Minor, and belongs to the Ignatian tradition in theology. His great work, *Against Heresies*, is not only a refutation of Gnosticism, but is also a positive exposition of Christian doctrine on the triple foundation of Creed, tradition and the Scriptures of both Testaments. More than any other Father of the Church Irenæus determined the general theological scheme within which the doctrines of the Trinity and the Incarnation were finally shaped. The significant thing about his theology is that he had a total view of Christianity. He begins from the principles of Ignatius, but he incorporates also the Logos philosophy of the Apologists, and makes large use of the Scriptures: above all, guided by tradition, he works the credal articles into his scheme.

Like Ignatius, he is not satisfied to present Christianity as a revealed moral religion: he finds in it also a religion of redemption, and in this way meets the Gnostic challenge as the Apologetic theology taken by itself could not do. He sets the true religion of redemption over against the Gnostic dualism. Creation and Redemption are the work of one and the same God. The key-word in the theology of Irenæus is recapitulation (ἀνακεφαλαίωσις: cp. Justin and Eph. i. 10). Justin had partly anticipated the Irenæan use of it (cp. Irenæus, *Adv. Hær.*, IV; 6, 2; Justin, *Dial.*, 100); but Irenæus develops the conception into a large theology. What he puts into the word recapitulation is a combination of the Pauline doctrine of the Second Adam with the Johannine doctrine of the Logos as the light and life of men. Christ in His Incarnation, Passion and Resurrection, not only brings the knowledge of God, but also undoes the sin of Adam and communicates to men moral renewal and, above all, incorruption or immortality. As Irenæus puts it, He recapitulates the first Creation, taking up the development of mankind where it was broken off by Adam's fall, and becoming the Head of a new humanity united to God and possessed of incorruption.

The work of Christ thus includes the sanctification of humanity, but the emphasis is on the impartation of immortality. Here we meet with the conception of 'deification', which dominates the later Greek theology. Irenæus says: 'Unless man had been united to God, he could not have been made partaker of incorruptibility' (*Adv. Hær.*, III, 18, 7); 'In no other way could we receive incorruption and immortality, except first we had been united to incorruption and immortality' (*ib.*, III, 19, 1); 'Jesus Christ in His immeasurable love was made what we are, that He might make us completely what He is' (*ib.*, V, Præf.). What Irenæus thus expresses is gathered up in the later Greek theology into the doctrine that man is 'deified' through the Incarnation, where it is especially the impartation of incorruption that is meant: this is known to modern scholars as the doctrine of 'physical redemption'. It is important to observe, however, that though Irenæus, developing suggestions of Ignatius, is the great author of the doctrine, his teaching is not limited to it. He continues also the spiritual Johannine view that the knowledge of God is itself incorruption (*Adv. Hær.*, IV, 20, 2; 36, 7; cp. Jn. xvii. 3).

It is from the point of view of the above doctrine of redemption that Irenæus deals with the Trinity. He stands to begin with on the identity of Son and Logos, using the words interchangeably. The Logos was eternally with the Father and revealed Him from the beginning (*Adv. Hær.*, II, 30, 9). The Father is the invisibility of the Son, the Son is the visibility of the Father (IV, 6, 6). Irenæus recognizes a twofold generation of the Son (III, 19, 2). The first generation is indescribable (II, 28, 6). Here Irenæus, like the later Fathers uses Isa. liii. 8: 'His generation who shall declare?' He says further that it was the Logos who was the subject of the Old Testament theophanies (IV. 20, 10), not the invisible God Himself. The Son and the Spirit are the two hands of God, to whom He said 'Let us make man' (IV, Præf.). Both are the offspring of God: to them all the angels are subject (IV. 7, 4).

A good deal here comes from the Apologists. But the whole is worked up into the Ignatian scheme of the dispensation or economy; in other words, the plan of salvation through the Incarnation. Irenæus says: 'The Logos of the Father and the Spirit of God, united to the ancient substance of Adam's creation, produced the living and perfect man receiving the perfect Father' (V, 1, 3). The Spirit prepares man for the Son of God, the Son leads him to the Father, and the Father bestows on him life eternal through the vision of God (IV, 20, 5).

What then of the second generation? How did Irenæus conceive of the Incarnation? In some passages it is clearly the Logos that is the subject in the historical Christ. It is so in the great fundamental saying, already quoted: 'He was made what we are, that He might make us completely what He is' (V, Præf.). So also it was the Logos Himself that hung on the Cross (V, 18, 1). But at the same time a distinction is made between the Logos and the man in the Incarnation. The Logos has no share in the sufferings of the man. He is quiescent in his temptation and dishonouring, crucifixion and death; but He helps the man in his victory and endurance, resurrection and ascension (III, 19, 3). Here the 'man' appears to have

F

an individuality of his own over against the Logos. Thus in the end Irenæus does not arrive at a firm decision as to how the Person of the historical Christ is to be conceived.

To sum up, Irenæus is a Biblical theologian, who is happier in quotation from the Scriptures than in using philosophical terminology. But he has adopted the Logos doctrine of the Apologists, so that they become an authentic source for Catholic Christianity in the struggle to define the doctrine of the Trinity. What is most important of all, however, in considering the theology of Irenæus, is that he transmits the Ignatian tradition; and that it is this tradition that gives him his outlook in searching the Scriptures.

3. TERTULLIAN

After Irenæus comes Tertullian, almost if not quite as important as a founder of the Ancient Catholic Church, and peculiarly important in the shaping of the doctrines of the Trinity and Incarnation. But short as is the distance in time between Irenæus who died *c.* A.D. 200, and Tertullian who died *c.* A.D. 225, the period was long enough to produce some change in the theological situation. Tertullian is not only an Antignostic Father, but is also a trenchant and potent adversary of what is known as Modalist Monarchianism. It will be proper, therefore, at this stage to say something about Monarchianism, of which there were two very different species. They are classed together, however, under the common head of Monarchianism, because each in its way was supremely interested in the unity of God.

The separation of the Gnostics from the Catholic Church did not at once solve the problems they had started. In fact the very means adopted to controvert the Gnostics led to further discussions. Appeal had been made to the Creed, tradition and the Scriptures. There now appeared a type of Christology which was based on the assertion that tradition pointed to a different interpretation of Creed and Scriptures from that of Irenæus. Mention has been made already of the Alogi who objected to the Logos philosophy and rejected the gospel of John. A still more determined attack was made upon the Logos doctrine by Theodotus, a learned man who came to Rome from Byzantium about A.D. 190. Eusebius tells us in his *Church History* (V, 28) that Theodotus said that Christ was a 'mere man' (ψιλὸς ἄνθρωπος), and that he supported this view by the assertion that it was the original teaching of the Apostles and the primitive Church. Theodotus accepted the Virgin birth and held Jesus to have been endowed with Divine powers at His baptism. Though he was not himself willing to call Jesus God, some of his followers admitted the title for Him after the Resurrection.

Historians have called this school or sect by the name of Dynamistic Monarchianism; Monarchianism, because it emphasized the monarchy or sole sovereignty of the One God; Dynamist, because it regarded Jesus as endowed with Divine power (δύναμις). The idea was clearly to return to the original *kerygma* and disallow the Pauline-Johannine developments. These Monarchians met Scriptural arguments directed against them by a demand for syllogistic argument; in other words they demanded rational coherence in interpretation. Eusebius even charges them with falsifying the Scriptures, so as to adapt them to their purpose.

These Dynamistic Monarchians are important, because the problem they raised is a real one. The original *kerygma* was very different from the subsequent Pauline-Johannine theology. But, as we have seen, in applying to Christ words used in the Old Testament of JAHWEH, it did contain the germ at least of the higher Christology: some of the followers of Theodotus seem to have perceived this. It should be added that the name connected later on with this early Dynamistic Monarchianism in the

West is not that of Theodotus, its originator, but is that of Artemon, who came to Rome *c.* A.D. 230.

So much then for Dynamistic Monarchianism. But there was in Tertullian's time also another type of Monarchianism, which gave still more trouble to the Catholic Church, since it found many sympathizers even amongst those who stood on Creed and Scripture. This was what has been called Modalist Monarchianism: its adherents held that the One God, remaining in Himself the same, successively manifested Himself under different aspects as Father, Son and Holy Spirit. Tertullian says that this doctrine was popular among the simple, who formed the largest part of the Church; it seemed to them the best way of protecting Monotheism against ditheistic or tritheistic corruption. It found at least partial favour with some of the Roman bishops of the early second century. There were several Modalist teachers in Rome about this time. One was Praxeas, against whom Tertullian wrote. But the man whose name was for ever afterwards associated with the doctrine was Sabellius: it is always called by later writers Sabellianism. He was excommunicated by Callistus, bishop of Rome A.D. 217–222. Information as to the precise doctrine of Sabellius is scanty; but Athanasius says that he taught that 'the Same was at one time Father, and at another Son of Himself' (*Or. contra Arianos*, III, 4); he also says that the Sabellians called God υἱοπάτωρ, i.e. Father and Son in One (*Expos. Fidei*). Pseudo-Athanasius in *Or. c. Ar.*, IV, 25 adds the Holy Spirit as the third form taken by the One God according to the Sabellian teaching.

Callistus, who excommunicated Sabellius, himself was a Monarchianist, who put forward a formula in which he sought to reconcile the two types of Monarchianism. According to Hippolytus (as quoted from *Philos.*, IX, 12 by Harnack, *Dogmengeschichte*, I⁴, p. 749, n. 2), Callistus maintained that the same Spirit was both Logos or Son and Father: this Spirit becoming incarnate in the Virgin deified the flesh He assumed, and made it One with Himself. Then what is seen is called the Son, and what is unseen the Father, 'so that Father and Son are called One God, and this Individual (πρόσωπον) being One cannot be two, and thus the Father suffered together with the Son'.

A special importance of this passage is that in it the word πρόσωπον appears for the first time in Christian theology. The word originally meant 'face'; then 'a mask', and so 'a dramatic character'; but here it seems just to stand for 'an individual'. It is not the precise equivalent of its apparent Latin synonym, *persona*, which came in with Tertullian; nor did it become the technical term in the usage of the Greek Fathers to express what Tertullian meant by *persona*. The technical term used for this was ὑπόστασις (*hypostasis*), which was brought in by Origen: πρόσωπον was, however, used as a non-technical equivalent for ὑπόστασις.

Finally, the later Fathers all agree that the Sabellians reduced the Godhead to one πρόσωπον, appearing under different names; when Basil represents their doctrine as a doctrine of three πρόσωπα, that is his way of attacking it, not a reproduction of actual Sabellian teaching. [See G. L. Prestige, *God in Patristic Thought*, p. 161.]

Tertullian lived from about A.D. 120 to 225. So far he has been considered along with Irenæus as an Antignostic Father and founder of the Ancient Catholic Church. But we now have to see the ways in which he differs from his predecessor. The greatest difference of all lies in the fact that he had no total view of Christianity such as Irenæus had. His works are occasional, and are conditioned by the particular purpose for which they were written. He wrote both Apologetic and Antignostic treatises; but the work which contains his important contribution to the doctrines of the Trinity and Incarnation was written against the Modalist Praxeas; strangely enough this was after he had become a Montanist. His special gift is in coining precise formulæ. Before his conversion to Christianity he had been a Roman jurist, and he carries with him into his theological work all his legal precision. No one has exercised more influence on the actual shape taken by the doctrine of the Trinity than Tertullian, except only Origen. Tertullian has greatly influenced the doctrine of the Incarnation also.

Another difference of Tertullian from Irenæus is to be seen in their relation to the Apologists. Tertullian stands much nearer to them than does the older theologian. He had been educated in the Stoic philosophy, one evidence of which is his curious doctrine that God, though a Spirit, is at the same time a body, as is also the human soul. But this was an eccentricity in Christian theology. It is more important that in his earlier period especially he often, under the influence of Stoicism, shares the Apologists' view of Christianity as a rational religion. But this rationalism is balanced by a strong regard for authority, which came naturally to the Roman jurist. The Rule of Faith is the law, on obedience to which salvation depends. No philosophy may compete with it, and it has priority even over the searching of the Scriptures.

We need not concern ourselves with Tertullian's attempts to interpret the Trinity which belong to his earlier, chiefly Apologetic, phase. In them he did not attain to the clearness which marks the great work against Praxeas. In it Tertullian says that he is following ancient tradition together with the higher Montanist instruction of the Paraclete. The continuation of the line of Ignatius and Irenæus is obvious. This is the book that has influenced posterity.

Tertullian begins with the unity of God and the idea

of dispensation, which he says the Greeks call economy (ὸικονομία). He develops the idea of the economy in a way that owes something to the Apologists, but is even more his own. The mystery of the economy disposes the Unity into a Trinity (*Adv. Praxeam,* 3). Tertullian is the first to use the Latin word *trinitas,* though Theophilus had already used the Greek equivalent τριάς.

The Trinity consists of Father, Son and Spirit, three not in *status,* but in degree (*ib.,* 2). Before the Creation of the world God possessed His Reason within Him, which at first contained the Spirit also within Itself (*ib.,* 5, 7). The Greeks call the Divine Reason λόγος, the Latins have been accustomed to use *sermo* (Word) as the translation of λόγος; but there is a distinction. God was always rational, but did not at first put forth His Reason in His Word (*ib.,* 5). This took place at the Creation, when 'even as the Paraclete teaches, God put forth His Word, as the root the stem, and the source the river, and the sun the ray' (*ib.,* 8). In this way we can speak of God and His Word as the Father and the Son who is the offspring of the Father. Further, there are here Two, God and His Word, the Father and His Son, yet they are no more divided than root and stem, source and river, sun and ray.

What then of the Spirit? When the Word was born by the will of the Father, the Spirit was immanent in the Word (*ib.,* 7, 27). Even in the Incarnation the Word and the Spirit were still undivided: the distinct existence of the Spirit began when the exalted Christ poured out the gift which He had received from the Father, 'the Holy Spirit, the third name in the Godhead' (*ib.,* 30). And so the Trinity is complete. The Spirit is third from the Father and the Son, 'as the fruit from the stem is third from the root, and the stream from the river is third from the source, and the point of the ray is third from the sun' (*ib.,* 8). Thus, if there are Two where there is a second, there are Three where there is a third. The Unity of God (*monarchia*) is preserved, since there is no separation; but the economy also is guarded, all the more that finally the Son returns His authority to the Father (I Cor. xv. 24).

Elsewhere in his book against Praxeas, Tertullian explains the Trinity in a different way. He speaks of the *monarchia* as administered through proximate Persons, the Son and the Spirit, these obtaining the second and third place, as consorts of the Substance of the Father, so that God appears to undergo division and dispersion (*ib.* 3). In this form of speech the emphasis is on the distinction of the Persons, although they share in the unity of the Substance. Whereas in the early *Apologeticus* (21) Tertullian had spoken of the Father and the Son as '*unus ambo*' (as we might say perhaps 'one Person'), now in the *Adversus Praxean* (25) he says of Father, Son and Spirit '*qui tres unum sunt, non unus*': they are one Substance, not one Person. The Persons are sufficiently distinct in Tertullian's mind for him to illustrate his meaning of their character by a reference to passages in Scripture where the Persons speak to one another, e.g. Ps. ii. 7.

It has been supposed that 'substance' and 'person' in Tertullian's discussion are to be interpreted by means of their use in Roman Law, where *substantia* can mean property, and *persona* one who has legal rights and obligations. But it is clear from Tertullian's further use of the terms that substance means concrete being (he gives the examples of stone and iron in *De Anima*, 32), while his use of *persona* is limited by the subject-matter. The word meant originally (1) a mask, (2) a character in a play, (3) the part any one sustains in the world, (4) a human being who sustains the part: the legal use (5) is a special application of (4). It is obvious that *persona* is a word of multiple suggestion. In *Adv. Prax.*, 25, Tertullian speaks of the 'Persons' as cohering in the unity of the Substance. He roundly denies that he means to speak of two Gods (*ib.*, 13).

The truth is that Tertullian is in two minds at once, as comes clearly to view in *Adv. Prax.*, 9. On the one hand, he says, 'The Father is the whole substance, but the Son is a derivative and portion of the whole.' Yet the Father is one, and the Son is another; and the Spirit makes a third. In fact, he goes on, things have to be named as they are, and some confusion of words cannot be avoided because of the nature of the matters spoken of.

Tertullian has succeeded admirably in doing two things. One is that he has clearly exhibited the problem of the Trinity in his attempt to combine identity and distinction. The other is that he has supplied the terms 'One Substance' and 'Three Persons', in which the subject has been discussed for centuries in Western theology.

The test of a doctrine of the Trinity being not only how it conserves the unity of God, but also how it explains the Incarnation, we proceed to see what Tertullian has done in this matter. Once more here too he has produced a precise terminology which prescribed the pattern for future discussion, though this time with a considerable modification of his technical terms. He makes use once more of the terms *substantia* and *persona*, but this time with an inversion of their position. Whereas in the doctrine of the Trinity he spoke of One Substance and three Persons, now he speaks of One Person and two substances. The Person is the Person of the Son or Logos Incarnate, and the substances are what were later called His Divine and human 'natures', in accordance with Origen's terminology. Paul had spoken of Christ as the Son of David according to the flesh, but the Son of God according to the Spirit. Tertullian translates this distinction of flesh and Spirit in Christ into that of the two substances in the One Person, each substance performing its proper operation, so that the Spirit remains impassible when the flesh perishes in death (*Adv. Prax.*, 27). But because of the unity of Christ's Person, Tertullian can say 'God was born' and 'the Son of God died' (*ib.*, 27, 29). Yet over against the Modalists he makes the distinction that these things happened according to the human substance. The phraseology, moreover, implies that the Logos is the subject in the historical Christ. It is to be observed that Tertullian, like Irenæus, sometimes speaks differently, giving more independence to the humanity. Thus (*ib.*, 27) he writes of God and the man Jesus as joined in One Person, and (*ib.*, 30) he says with reference to Mt. xxvii. 46 that God forsook the Son when He delivered over to death 'the man appertaining to Him' (*hominem ejus*).

A word in conclusion on Tertullian's achievement. It may be thought that there is inconsistency in emphasizing the precision of his terminology, when he himself speaks of an inevitable confusion in applying words to describe the Trinity. There is no inconsistency. The terms are precise, the meaning is not. Both in the doctrine of the Trinity and in that of the Incarnation it is now the Unity and now the distinctions that prevail. One may say that the theological battles of the next centuries turn on the attempt to interpret Tertullian's terms, or their Greek equivalents, in such a way as to fit them for the work they were required to do. Only in saying this it must be remembered that the Greek substitutes were not exact equivalents, and so a further complication was introduced into the doctrinal process. It was in fact dominated by the Greek forms of thought, and yet from time to time suffered a reaction of Tertullian's conceptions upon it.

Novatian's *De Trinitate* (*c.* A.D. 250, epitomized Tertullian's doctrine with little change. Tertullian's economic view of the Trinity continued to influence Western thought even as late as the fourth century. His doctrine of the Person of Christ had a still more lasting influence.

4. ORIGEN

Clement of Alexandria (d. before A.D. 216) is also reckoned as an Antignostic Father along with Irenæus and Tertullian; and such indeed he is, though his answer to Gnosticism is of a very different kind from that of either of the others. Instead of opposing to Gnosticism a theology based on Creed, tradition and Scripture, Clement strove to outbid the heretical Gnosis by means of a Catholic Gnosis, related to the common faith of the Church as a higher stage to which the 'perfect' might attain. He proposed in fact to do for Christianity what Philo had done for Judaism, that is to transform it into an esoteric philosophical religion. But as Clement did not oppose the common faith of the Church, as did the heretical Gnostics, he remained within its communion. His position was made possible by the fact that older conditions lasted longer in Alexandria than in the West, so that there was much less definition of standards. The Canon of the two Testaments was authoritative in Alexandria as elsewhere, but the bishop was less sharply separated from the presbyters than in the West, and when Clement speaks of a Christian confession he seems to mean something altogether less precise than the Roman creed. In the East in general there was variation in the baptismal confession from church to church; and the Christian faith long meant for Oriental Christians, not a definite formula, but the substance of Scripture teaching.

This common faith, as held by the ordinary un-philosophical majority of Christians, is Clement's starting point. It is the lower stage, from which the higher level of knowledge (Gnosis) can be reached. The aim of Clement's writings is to show how this is possible. His religious philosophy or Gnosis resembles the doctrine of the second century Apologists. God is absolutely transcendent, and is revealed through the Logos. It is He who gave philosophy to the Greeks and the law to the Jews, and who finally, as manifested in Christ, leads up from faith to knowledge. It is just in this last point that Clement modifies the Apologetic teaching. The Apologists on the whole left the common faith uninterpreted except for the addition to it of their Logos doctrine. Clement intends that, for those who can bear it, the common faith should pass over into a knowledge which is not merely the moralism of the Apologists, but is rather a religion of grace in which the Logos communicates Himself to the heart, conferring the freedom which obeys the law spontaneously out of love.

Clement's real importance is not in his treatment of particular doctrines, where he suffers from vagueness; but is in the stimulus which he gave to his great scholar Origen, who sought to carry out in detail the scheme that Clement had proposed.

Origen (A.D. 185–254) first taught in Alexandria, and then founded a theological school at Cæsarea in Palestine. He differs from Clement, not only in being more scientific, but also in being more ecclesiastical. He was nearer to Western Christianity in that he recognized a definite Rule of Faith, though he did not take it from a creed, but stated it in his *De Principiis* in his own language. He gave great attention to the Scriptures, on which the greater part of his works are commentaries.

He differed also from Clement in another way in that he was contemporary with, and was influenced by, a new philosophical movement, which in Clement's time was only just beginning and had not yet attained to clarity. This new philosophy was Neoplatonism. It was, to be sure, only a further development of Greek thought along the lines already struck out in Neopythagoreanism. But in the hands of Plotinus, Origen's contemporary, it became a great coherent system, speculative and scientific at the same time; it was indeed the final magnificent bloom on the tree of Greek philosophy. It is necessary now to touch upon this system, since when Origen after the example of Clement seeks to transform faith into knowledge, the particular form of Gnosis at which he aims is influenced, not by the eclectic, principally Stoic, philosophy that ruled in the time of the Apologists, but by the newer philosophy of his own century. According to Eusebius' *Church History* (VI., 19) Origen studied under Ammonius Saccas, the originator of Neoplatonism, who was also the master of Plotinus. Ammonius left nothing in writing, so that we do not know precisely what Origen received from him. But for our purposes it is sufficient to put into comparison with Origen's theology a brief outline of Neoplatonism as expounded by his contemporary Plotinus.

The system of that philosopher began like Neopythagoreanism with the One that is beyond all Being and all Thought. From the One emanate in a descending scale the Nous and the World-Soul. The Nous, the Image of the One, is at once Thought and the Universe of Ideas contained therein. The World-Soul transforms the Ideas of the Nous into active principles. From the World-Soul all individual souls are derived. These include both gods and men. It is noteworthy that Plotinus speaks of the One, the Nous and the World-Soul as the three primary hypostases (ὑποστάσεις). (We defer further detailed discussion of the term 'hypostasis' till we meet it in the theology of Origen. It is enough now to recall that its general meaning is 'substance', as in Heb. xi. 1, R.V.) To continue: Lower than Soul is Body, and lowest of all is Matter, the extreme opposite of the One. Matter is properly Non-Being, though at the same time it is the potentiality of all becoming. Out of it the World-Soul forms its body, the sensible World, and the individual souls form their particular bodies. While those of the gods are bodies of light (the stars), those of men are gross. In short for them body is a prison, whence they desire to return to the One, from which ultimately they emanate. The way of return has three stages. The first is purification from the bonds of sense; the second is contemplation of the Ideas forming the content of the Nous; the third and final stage is union with the One in an ecstasy where all distinction between the soul and the One vanishes. It will be seen that Neoplatonism is a religious philosophy. It may be regarded as the final effort of pagan philosophy to simplify and clear itself so as to become a gospel.

And now for Origen's philosophical theology, or Christian Gnosis, which amalgamates the elements of the Rule of Faith, as he conceived them, with the principles of Neoplatonism in a system which, while it shows its derivation from both, is a highly original creation. Irenæus had a total view of Christianity, Tertullian worked out individual doctrines and provided precise formulæ, Clement had an idea which Origen developed. But none of the three has a real system such as Origen offers. His doctrine is the first complete Christian theology; and as such it exercised a very great influence upon the theologians who followed him: they partly adopted his conceptions, and partly reacted from them.

Origen's system is contained in his work *De Principiis* (περὶ ἀρχῶν), which has four books. The first three contain the theology proper, while the fourth is devoted to showing how Scriptural language may be interpreted from a theological point of view. The method of removing difficulties is that of allegorical interpretation, by means of which Scripture and philosophical theology can be harmonized.

Unfortunately the *De Principiis* is extant for the most

part only in the Latin translation of Rufinus, who admits in his Preface that he has altered some passages so as to bring all into accord with Origen's best thought; he says that he has inserted nothing that is not genuinely Origenistic, but that inconsistencies have been removed. Rufinus (d. A.D. 410) had behind him the Arian controversy, which originated out of different developments from Origen's theology, as we shall see presently. Here it will be sufficient to anticipate so far as to say that Arianism was a doctrine which carried subordination in the Trinity to the extent of maintaining that the Father alone is truly God, and that the Logos was a creature, originating in time and mutable like other creatures. The Arians said of the Logos: 'There was when He was not.' Rufinus was anxious to remove from his translation whatever might appear to favour Arianism, and to leave only what was against it. It is possible, however, to check the work of Rufinus to a considerable extent. On the one hand, Athanasius in his *De Decretis* (*c*. A.D. 350) has recorded two passages from Origen of a definitely anti-Arian character, and he argues that these represent the considered opinion of 'the laborious man': where he wrote otherwise it was by way of enquiry and discussion only. But this defence of Origen only goes part of the way; for on the other hand, the Emperor Justinian, wishing to prove Origen a heretic, quotes strongly Arianizing passages from the now lost Greek text of the *De Principiis*, containing positive doctrinal statements which show how much Rufinus has done in the way of alteration. Justinian was writing to Menna, Patriarch of Constantinople (A.D. 548).

It is now time to turn to Origen himself. The first thing requisite is to note the new terminology that comes in with him. To begin with, there is the term *hypostasis* (ὑπόστασις), which corresponds to Tertullian's *persona*, but has a different connotation. It is now necessary to examine the meaning of the word in more detail than has been done previously. It means properly 'substratum', and then comes to mean subsistence or concrete existence. It is still further away from what we mean by personality, the mark of which is consciousness, than is Tertullian's *persona*. The use of *hypostasis* by Origen and the Fathers after him is carefully to be distinguished from its modern use in expounding the later Jewish theology, where it stands for the quasi-personification of a Divine attribute. The meaning in this use may approach the patristic usage on one side, but the whole connotation is different. The situation has been changed from that of Judaism by the new fact of the Incarnation.

We note next Origen's use of *ousia* (οὐσία), which just means 'being', but which he uses as an alternative for *hypostasis*, making no distinction such as was made later between the two terms.

Finally, where Tertullian speaks of two substances in the Person of Christ, Origen uses the more abstract phraseology of two 'natures' (φύσεις).

With these preliminary explanations, we go on to Origen's doctrine of the Trinity, as stated in the *De Principiis*. It is clear that he was acquainted with Tertullian's type of teaching, as he spends great labour in showing that God being Spirit cannot be a body. He is a simple intellectual nature, free from all composition. He is the Monad (μονάς), and so to speak, the Henad (ἑνάς), the One and Only Being, the source whence is the origin of the whole intellectual nature (*De Princ.*, I, 1). His works in nature are, as it were, rays from His Being; so that He can be perceived through their beauty. But, inasmuch as the Divine nature altogether exceeds all corporeal natures, God is revealed in Christ, who is His Image. Thus we come to the doctrine of the Son, who is both Divine and human: Origen treats first of His Divinity. The Only-Begotten Son of God is His Wisdom, substantially existing. Nothing more can properly be said of His incorporeal hypostasis or substance. It is because of the generation of His Wisdom that God is called Father (I, 2.2). It is impossible to compare the generation of the Son with that of men and animals. It is beyond human thought. It is an eternal generation like that of radiance from light (I, 2–4). There never was a time when the Divine Wisdom was not.

Further, in the summary of the doctrine of the Trinity in IV. 28 it is said that the Son is not generated from the Father by a putting forth (*prolatio*); nor is He any part of the substance of the Father. This statement is evidently aimed at Tertullian's doctrine, both as regards the putting forth of the Logos and His being a part of God's substance. The summary in fact goes on to say that the Son can no more be separated from the Father than His Word or His Wisdom or His Image, all of which mean the same thing. It is One Substance in which is the fulness of the Godhead. Even when we say that there never was when He was not (speaking of the Son), we have to remember that we are really speaking of what is beyond all time.

An important remark may be made on the above statement. It is that the fragments from Origen in Athanasius *De Decretis*, 27, fully justify as genuine Origenism the phraseology Rufinus gives us twice in the *De Principiis* (I, 2.9 and also IV, 28): 'there never was when the Son was not'—phraseology which already anticipates and contradicts the Arian shibboleth of the fourth century: 'There was when He was not.'

To the same side of Origen's teaching as that which we have been studying belongs a fragment from his Commentary on the Epistle to the Hebrews [Lommatzsch: *Origenis Opera*, V, p. 300]. Here Origen refers to the 'Wisdom of Solomon', vi, 25, which teaches by the simile of 'breath' that proceeds from bodily substance, how Wisdom similarly proceeds from the very substance of God. The second simile of 'effluence' (ἀπόρροια) has the

G

same import. It shows a communion of substance between the Father and the Son. In fact 'effluence' implies that the Son is of the same substance (ὁμοούσιος) with the Father. Here apparently is the first appearance of the term which later became the key-word of the Creed of Nicæa.

There was, however, strongly contrasted with the foregoing, another aspect of Origen's doctrine, as is clear from the fragments of the original Greek preserved in Justinian's letter to Menna. These fragments are evidence of an inferiorism which has disappeared in the translation of Rufinus. They are given in Redepenning's edition of the *De Principiis*.

I quote as follows: Bk. I, Fragment 6: 'We are persuaded that everything whatever except the Father and God of the Universe is originate (γενητόν).'

Bk. I, Fragment 5: 'It would be right to say that the Saviour is an Image of God's goodness, but is not good of Himself (ἀυτοαγαθός). The Son may be called good, but not simply good. He is the Image of the Invisible God, and so may be called God (Θεός, without the article, meaning "Divine"), but not in the sense that Christ Himself speaks of the only God (Jn. xvii. 3): thus He is an Image of God's goodness, but not unchangeably good.'

Bk. IV, Fragment 5: 'Now this the Son is begotten of the will of the Father, who is the Image of the Invisible God and the effluence of His glory, the representation of His substance (ὑποστάσεως), the firstborn of all creation, a creature (κτίσμα), Wisdom. For Wisdom herself says: God created (ἔκτισε) me as the beginning of His ways unto His works.'

All these passages are strongly subordinationist. What is said in Bk. I, Fragment 5, may be further illustrated from Origen's Commentary on Jn. II. 2, where he points out (in explaining the first verse of the Gospel), that there is a difference between ὁ Θεός with the article, meaning God, and Θεός without the article, meaning

Divine. He says that God Himself alone is ὁ Θεός and αὐτο-Θεός (God of Himself): everything else is deified by participation of His Godhead. The Logos, therefore, is fitly called not ὁ Θεός, but Θεός simply.

Origen in the above passages quoted by Justinian thinks in fact of the Divine Logos or Wisdom very much as Plotinus thinks of the Nous. In *Contra Celsum*, III, 39, he says that Jesus is a mediator between the nature of the unoriginate and all that is originate. And in his Commentary on Jn. I. 39 he writes that the Divine Wisdom 'is the incorporeal hypostasis of a variety of contemplations, which contain the reasons (λόγοι) of all things'.

When we come to Origen's doctrine of the Holy Spirit the subordinationism and inferiorism are even more marked. It is true that in *De Principiis*, I, 3.5, he says that the Trinity is not whole without the Holy Spirit, and in IV, 35 we read (in the translation of Rufinus) that 'there is nothing that was not made except the nature of the Father and the Son and the Holy Spirit'. Further, in his expanded statement of the Rule of Faith (I, Præf.), Origen says that the Spirit is associated with the Father and the Son in honour and dignity. But he goes on to say (according to Rufinus) that the Rule does not determine clearly whether he was 'born or not born' (γεννητός ἢ ἀγέννητος); while Jerome quoting the same passage has 'made or not made' (γενητὸς ἢ ἀγένητος). This makes us ask: How much has Rufinus done in modifying the text? Justinian's Fragment, Bk. I, 8 is strongly inferioristic with regard to the Holy Spirit. Origen writes as follows: 'The God and Father who holds all things together, reaches by His influence each one of the things that are, bestowing being upon each from what is His own. One of these things is the Son who is less than the Father, and whose influence reaches to rational beings only, for He is second from the Father. Still inferior is the Holy Spirit, who penetrates only the saints; so that

in this way the power of the Father is greater than that
of the Son, but that of the Son is more than that of the
Holy Spirit.'

It will be observed that the above quotation, including
the Son as well as the Spirit, presents a subordinationist
doctrine of the Trinity as a whole. With it may be compared an important passage in the Commentary on
Jn. II. 6, where Origen says: 'We are persuaded that there
are three hypostases, the Father, the Son and the Holy
Spirit and we believe that there is none other unbegotten
being than the Father, and we approve as the more
reverent and the true opinion, that of all things made
through the Logos, the Holy Spirit is more honourable
than all others and ranks above all other things made by
the Father through Christ.' With the above passages
entirely agrees Justinian's assertion in his Epistle to
Menna; Origen said 'that the Son and the Holy Spirit
are creatures (κτίσματα)'. [Lommatzsch: *Origenis Opera*,
XXII, p. 179.]

Thus when Rufinus represents Origen as writing in
De Princ., I, 3.7: 'Nothing in the Trinity is to be called
greater or less', this seems beyond justification, even if
we know from Athanasius that he did say of the Logos,
'there never was when He was not'.

The reconciliation in Origen's mind of the eternal
generation of the Logos and the inferiorism in the Trinity
is to be found in the fact that for him all spiritual beings
are eternal. Thus the eternity of the Son and the Spirit
can coexist with an inferiorism of both as compared with
the Father, who alone is truly God. The difference of the
Son and the Spirit from other spirits is not in their
eternal origination, but in the fact that all spirits below
the Trinity have declined from the good, the soul of
Jesus only excepted. As a punishment they are incar-
cerated in material bodies, matter having been created
for the purpose. The Logos brings redemption by His

Incarnation, uniting Himself to a soul that has remained pure in its pre-existence. In Jesus Divine and human nature (φύσις) began to be united. As a result human nature by communion with what is more divine, itself becomes divine in all who in faith take up the life which Jesus taught (*contra Celsum*, III, 28). It has been mentioned already more than once that Origen's φύσις in its application to the Incarnation is equivalent to Tertullian's *substantia* in this reference. Like Tertullian Origen sharply distinguishes the properties of the two natures. The Logos remaining the same in essence suffers nothing of what the body or soul suffers (*Contra Celsum*, IV, 15).

The consummation of all is in the future life. Whereas Irenæus and Tertullian had maintained with the Creed the resurrection of the flesh, Origen spiritualizes the primitive Christian eschatology. All spirits will ultimately return to God. Nothing material will be left.

Origen's system marks a turning point in the history of Christian doctrine. The Hellenization of the primitive *kerygma* was begun by Paul, the author of Hebrews, and the writer of the Fourth Gospel. It was carried by the second-century Apologists to a point where much New Testament Christianity remained only as unscientific tradition. Irenæus and Tertullian using the Creed and the Scriptures sought to interpret the tradition so as to bring it to the level of the scientific Apologetic theology. Clement of Alexandria proposed a way by which the traditional faith might be treated as a preliminary stage towards a scientific theology more Christian than that of the Apologists. Origen in the end has absorbed everything into one grandiose system, and so has completed the Hellenization of Christianity. The question raised by subsequent theology was, had he gone too far? The work of the later Greek Fathers on the Trinity and the Incarnation might well be summed up as a criticism of Origen, in which they sought to separate what they thought precious from what they regarded as vile. To begin with, Origenism dominated Eastern theology; but the day came when the great theologian was adjudged a heretic. Even then, however, his influence did not cease to work. It worked in the continual interpretation of Scripture by theology, even if the theological system adopted was no longer pure Origenism.

5. THE ADVANCE AND RETROCESSION OF ORIGENISM

The first triumph of Origenism was a victory over Monarchianism in the East. Both Dynamistic and Modalist Monarchianism existed there in Origen's own lifetime. As in the West simple Christians had disliked the Logos doctrine, so now in the East they were repelled by the doctrine of the hypostases (*Contra Celsum*, VIII, 12): it seemed to them to imperil faith in the unity of God. A modalistic doctrine of the Trinity appeared to them the safer way of thinking. But after Origen had done his work, such doctrine was regarded by representative theologians as Sabellian heresy. Dynamistic Monarchianism was less common in the East than Modalism; but it gave much more trouble to the Origenists, as it found an outstanding and remarkable representative in Paul of Samosata, bishop of Antioch from about A.D. 260. He was condemned as a heretic at a Council held in Antioch about A.D. 268.

Paul is an enigmatic figure. Only imperfect remains of his teaching have been preserved by those who repudiated it. All we have bears on his Christology: we know nothing about his views otherwise. The most important Pauline fragments are from what is left of the synodical letter condemning his doctrine, and from notes of a disputation with the Origenist presbyter Malchion, who was the chief inquisitor at the Council. These fragments are collected in the exhaustive treatise of Loofs, 'Paul of Samosata', in *Texte und Untersuchungen*, Bk. XLIV, 1924, pp. 330–7. Loofs also includes fragments from the Λόγοι πρὸς Σαβῖνον, ascribed to Paul, which are of more doubtful value, p. 339; while on p. 338 he gives fragments of Pauline doctrine, quoted from Paul's followers by the heresiologist Epiphanius, who wrote on heresies A.D. 374–377.

What is clear about Paul is that he stood for a revised Christology, which had important implications for the doctrine of the Trinity. Eusebius quotes the following verdict of his judges in the Synodical letter: 'He will not confess with us that the Son of God descended from heaven.' The Council took Paul's objection to the popular Christology to mean that he held Christ to be a mere man (ψιλὸς ἄνθρωπος); and they accused him of reviving the heresy of Artemon.

A review of Paul's doctrine in Pseudo-Athanasius, *Contra Apollinarem*, II, 3, though written by an adversary, is more discerning of Paul's intention. It was to show the immanence of God in the human Jesus. We read: 'Paul of Samosata confesses God originating from the Virgin, God appearing from Nazareth, having taken thence the beginning both of His existence and His reign, while the Word in whom was Wisdom was efficacious in working from heaven. Jesus was fore-ordained before all worlds, but was manifested in existence from Nazareth. This Paul says that God may be One, God over all, the Father.'

What we actually know of Paul's Christology from the fragments of the Synodical letter may be summarized as follows: What Mary bore was not the Logos, but a man like us, and the grace upon Him was from the Holy Spirit. It was the man Jesus who was anointed, not the Logos. But Wisdom, or the Logos, dwelt in Him as in no other. There was a conjunction (συνάφεια) between the man and the Logos. Jesus was formed primarily as man in the womb: in the second place, He was God coexistent with the humanity. The conjunction, however, took place not essentially (οὐσιωδῶς), but qualitatively (κατὰ ποιότητα): it was according to instruction and participation, not according to essence existent in the body (κατὰ μάθησιν καὶ μετουσίαν, οὐχὶ οὐσίαν οὐσιωμένην ἐν σώματι). Yet the conjunction was very close. Paul says: 'The God who wore and put on the humanity was not without participation in the sufferings which were primarily human; nor was the humanity, in which He was, without part in what was primarily Divine.'

So much for the Christology. What did it imply in Paul's mind with regard to the Trinity? Unfortunately here our information is inadequate. But there is a remarkable fragment from the disputation with Malchion which compares the origination of the Logos with that of Jesus. 'The Logos came together with Him who sprang from David, who is Jesus Christ begotten of Holy Spirit. And Him the Virgin bore through Holy Spirit, but the Logos God begat without Virgin or any other, there being none but God; and so the Logos subsisted (ὑπέστη).' We might paraphrase the last clause thus: 'and this was the origination of the hypostasis (ὑπόστασις) of the Logos', since noun and verb are from the same root. This passage suggests a distinction of the Logos from God. Nevertheless we know that Paul identified God and the Logos most closely. According to Epiphanius, the Pauline doctrine was: 'There is One Person (πρόσωπον) of God and the Logos (i.e. His Reason), as the man and his own Logos (or reason) are one.' But Jesus Christ is a second Person. We have from Epiphanius again: 'The Father with the Son is One God, but the man brings to light His Person in our world, and thus the two Persons are completed.'

Paul's doctrine may be regarded as another revolt of the original *kerygma* against the doctrine of Christ's pre-existence which had been added to it; but it is a more intelligent revolt than that of Theodotus and Artemon.

It denies pre-existence in the popular sense, but strives to reinterpret it so as to preserve Christ's humanity, which had been jeopardized by the doctrine that the Logos was the subject in the historical Christ. Paul's Christology is fairly clear, though we only have fragments of his teaching. Unfortunately his Trinitarian doctrine is not so clear. The net result of a combination of the Disputation fragment (above referred to) with the evidence from Epiphanius, seems to be that Paul, while acknowledging a hypostatic distinction in God, went to psychology for its explanation. If so, he anticipated not only some of the later Greek fathers, but still more Augustine and Aquinas.

Paul was condemned, and it was decided for orthodox theology that the subject in the historical Christ was the Logos. But the desire to assert a human subject came to life again in various ways, as we shall see. The Pauline Trinitarianism was opposed to the current of the time, and was apparently too sketchy to stand up against it. Its merit is in its suggestiveness, rather than in its accomplishment.

Athanasius, Basil and Hilary all tell us that the Council condemned Paul's use of the word ὁμοούσιος; but there is not agreement as to the reason why. The point is only of importance because the condemnation gave trouble later on, when the word became the watchword of orthodoxy.

So far then Origenism was victorious. But there were three obstacles militating against its complete triumph. The first of course was the internal contradiction in the system itself. The second was the continued persistence in the East of another doctrinal tradition, that of Ignatius and Irenæus, the third was that the West had a doctrine of its own, begun by Tertullian and continued by Novatian: this doctrine stood much nearer to Ignatius and Irenæus than to Origen.

Methodius, Bishop of Olympus (d. A.D. 311), illustrates the impact of the Irenæan tradition upon Origenism. He found the system contrary to the Rule of Faith, in that it taught (1) the eternity of all spirits, (2) the fall of all (except the Trinity) in the state of pre-existence and their incarceration in material bodies, and finally (3) the spiritualization of the resurrection in opposition to the Irenæan realism: this involved a different notion of deification in the two types of doctrine—for Irenæus it was spiritual and physical, for Origen spiritual only.

Such criticism had its impact upon the Origenists themselves; so that even a successor of his in the Alexandrian catechetical school, Peter, Bishop of Alexandria (d. A.D. 311), while under Origen's influence, yet abandoned the doctrines attacked by Methodius. This abandonment, however, made a breach in the system, and exposed to full view the internal contradiction which existed between the eternity of the three hypostases, and the inferiorism which made the Son, and still more the Spirit, each a creature (κτίσμα). This contradiction had indeed already been clearly disclosed, when Dionysius, Bishop of Alexandria (d. A.D. 264), a pupil of Origen, in attacking Sabellianism went to the opposite extreme in distinguishing the hypostases: he said not only that the Son was alien in essence from the Father, but also that as a thing made He was not before He came into existence. This brought down on him a reproof from Dionysius, Bishop of Rome (A.D. 259–268), who developed the Western doctrine as it had been formed by Tertullian and consolidated by Novatian. He maintains the Divine Monarchy and fulminates against the division of the sacred Monad into three hypostases, foreign to each other and utterly separate. The Divine Triad is gathered up into the One God of the Universe. It is a blasphemy to say that the Son ever was not: that would mean that once the Father was destitute of Word and Wisdom and Power. The new element here in which Dionysius of Rome goes beyond Tertullian and Novatian is in accepting the eternal generation of the Son which Origen had taught, but at the same time denying that ἔκτισε in Prov. viii. 22, LXX, meant 'created': the Son is not a thing made (ποίημα). The emphasis remains on the unity of the Word and the Holy Spirit with the God of the Universe. Thereby the Divine Triad and the Monarchia are equally preserved.

The Alexandrian bishop replied to his namesake, saying that he had never denied that Christ was of the same essence with God. He had used the images of root and plant, source and stream to explain the generation of the Son, pointing out that both unity and difference were implied.

The opinions of Dionysius of Alexandria are discussed by Athanasius in a special treatise, *De sententia Dionysii*, where Athanasius defends Dionysius, saying that he is not to be judged by one utterance in particular circumstances: he expressed himself quite differently at other times. In *De Decretis*, 26, Athanasius gives a long extract from a writing of Dionysius of Rome: this has been epitomized in the preceding paragraph.

6. THE ARIAN CONTROVERSY

The controversy between the two Dionysii was only a foretaste of the great debate which filled the fourth Christian century. It was once more the Origenist antagonism to Sabellianism that provoked the conflict. Arius, a presbyter of Alexandria, is said to have accused his bishop, Alexander, of that heresy. This was in A.D. 319. Alexander, though himself an Origenist, had revolted against the doctrine that the Son was a creature (κτίσμα), or a thing made (ποίημα), declaring that the Father was always Father and the Son always Son. (cp. Alexander's Encyclical letter in *Depositio Arii*, 3). Such views appeared to Arius to overthrow all that Origen had done to Hellenize Christianity. What Arius wanted was a doctrine that would explain the origin of the Universe in a way satisfactory to the Greek mind.

In his *Orations against the Arians*, I, 5, 6, and in his *De Synodis*, 15, Athanasius has recorded the opinions of Arius as expressed by himself in his *Thalia*, a metrical poem on the Trinity. Arius taught as follows: God in His own nature is ineffable and has no equal. He is called Ingenerate and Inoriginate in opposition to the Son, who is generated and who was the beginning of things originated. All things are through the Son, but to the Son, as to all other beings God is naturally invisible. The Son only sees the Father by a power granted from God (i.e. the Holy Spirit). Thus there is a Triad unequal in glory and separate and alien in their subsistences (ὑποστάσεις). All things being alien from and unlike to God, so also the Son is different from and unlike (ἀνόμοιος) in all respects to the essence (οὐσία) of the Father. The Logos is not true God. He partakes of God like all others, so that He is only called God in name. Far from being able to understand the Father, He does not even know His own essence.

There was a time when He was not, and He was not before His origination (ἦν ποτε ὅτι οὐκ ἦν, καὶ οὐκ ἦν πρὶν γένηται). God created Him for the purpose of creating us. He has therefore a pre-eminence over all other creatures, but He resembles them in that, like all below God Himself, He is mutable (τρεπτός), and can do either right or wrong. It is of His own will that He remains good.

In a Creed presented to Alexander (*De Synodis*, 16) Arius acknowledged the Father as the source of all things and denied that the Son was a part of the Father of the same essence (ὁμοούσιος) with Him, or was an offshoot (προβολή) from Him; such assertions amount to making the incorporeal God suffer in a body (i.e. undergo bodily division).

The view of Arius that the Logos was a creature and mutable enabled him to maintain that He was the subject in the historical Christ, and yet could experience growth and development (Lk. ii. 52), anxiety (Jn. xii. 27) and the fear of death (Mt. xxvi. 39). Arius taught that in Christ the Logos simply took the place of the human soul (Athanasius, *Orations*, III, 51–58).

The Hellenization of Christianity was a necessary process, if it was to be made intelligible to others than the Jews. Moreover, Greek philosophy provided the natural language in which its meaning could be explained. But all translation involves tension between the original and the transcript. With Arius the medium of explanation threatened to destroy the thing to be explained. The economy or plan of salvation, which Irenæus had summed up as deification, was at stake. In the language of Greek theology, the charge against Arianism is expressed by saying that the Logos of Arius could not deify, since He Himself was only deified by participation (Athanasius, *Or.*, I, 6). Nor could He communicate a true knowledge of God, since He can neither see nor know His own Father accurately. It may be added that the Arian doctrine did not save the humanity of Christ, since the Arian Christ was no more true man than true God.

The controversy that had begun between Arius and his bishop Alexander, after a number of preliminary moves, came to an issue at the great œcumenical Council of Nicæa, A.D. 325. An agreement had been reached already between Alexander and Hosius, bishop of Cordova, who had the ear of the Emperor Constantine, who himself called the Council in the interest of ecclesiastical peace, and also himself dominated it. Arius was condemned, and an anti-Arian creed was adopted.

This famous creed is, together with its anathemas, a landmark in the history of the doctrine of the Trinity. It is as follows:—

'We believe in One God, the Father Almighty, Maker of all things visible and invisible. And in One Lord Jesus Christ, the Son of God, begotten of the Father, only-begotten, that is of the essence (οὐσία) of the Father, God of God, Light of Light, true God of true God, begotten, not made, of one essence (ὁμοούσιον) with the Father, by whom all things were made, both the things in heaven and the things on earth: who for us men and for our salvation came down and was made flesh, was made man, suffered, and rose again on the third day, ascended into the heavens, and comes to judge the living and the dead. And (we believe) in the Holy Spirit.

"But those that say that there was a time when He was not, and that He was not before He was begotten, and that He was made out of nothing; or assert that He is of another hypostasis or essence (ἐξ ἑτέρας ὑποστάσεως ἢ οὐσίας), or is either created or mutable or variable (κτιστὸν ἢ τρεπτὸν ἢ ἀλλοιωτόν)—such the Catholic Church anathematizes.'

The Creed, as above, is given in the Epistle of Eusebius to his church in Cæsarea, to be found at the end of Athanasius *De Decretis*. From this letter we learn that the basis of the Creed of Nicæa was the baptismal creed of Cæsarea, put forward by Eusebius himself at the Council: he was a moderate Origenist. This Cæsarean creed is also given in the Epistle, and contains the following:

'We believe in One God, the Father Almighty, Maker of all things visible and invisible. And in One Lord Jesus Christ, the Word of God, God of God, Light of Light, Life of Life, Only-begotten Son, First born of all creation, begotten of the Father before all the ages, through whom also all things were made; who for our salvation was made man and lived among men, suffered and rose again on the third day and ascended to the Father, and will come again in glory to judge the living and the dead. And we believe in One Holy Spirit.'

Eusebius in his letter tells his people how after a purely Arian creed had been proposed and rejected, he himself brought forward his own creed of Cæsarea, and it was found generally acceptable. But Constantine, advised by Hosius, demanded that the Eusebian creed should be strengthened against Arianism by the addition of the word ὁμοούσιον, of the same essence, (the equivalent of the Latin *unius substantiæ*). The Council accepted this proposal and proceeded to rewrite the creed on the basis of it. 'Word' (Logos) in the creed of Cæsarea was replaced by 'Son'; only-begotten, firstborn of all creation becomes 'begotten of the Father, only-begotten, that is of the essence of the Father'. And just before the introduction of the key-word ὁμοούσιον there was added: 'true God of true God, begotten not made'. After this the clauses on Christ's saving work were amplified, and finally there were subjoined the anathemas against Arianism. In a word, not only had ὁμοούσιον been written into the creed, but also it had been buttressed on all sides with phrases intended to bring out its significance both as to what it asserts and what it denies.

In his letter Eusebius shows plainly that he did not like the changes. He objected to the ὁμοούσιον, till it was explained that it was put in to show that the Son was of the Father, but was not a part of the Father. This was good Origenism; so Eusebius accepted the new word, as he says, both for the sake of peace and for fear of declining from the truth (i.e. of Arianizing). He further admitted 'begotten not made', since 'made' applied to the creatures made through the Son, not to Himself who was not like them but was of a more excellent essence, being begotten of the Father by a mysterious generation, as the Scriptures teach.

Moreover, says Eusebius, it was made clear that the Son was of one essence with the Father, but not in the way that the phrase applies to inanimate bodies or animals or men. There is no division or separation of the Divine essence, nor is there any conversion or change of it: all such things are foreign to the ingenerate nature of the Father. In fact, the word ὁμοούσιον signifies that there is no likeness between the Son of God and things made. He is like in all respects only to the Father who begat Him, and is of no other hypostasis or essence. With these explanations Eusebius felt able to accept the ὁμοούσιον. He could even accept the anathemas in spite of their being novelties; they merely forbid phrases not found in Scripture.

Nothing could make clearer the difficulties of the moderate Origenists, when faced with the Nicene creed, than this letter of Eusebius to his church. They were willing to repudiate Arianism, but did not like the means adopted, notably the word ὁμοούσιον. When this word is put back into Latin, its origin is clear: it is simply the *unius substantiæ* of Tertullian and Novatian, long familiar in the West. But Alexander, and a few other Eastern bishops, saw in it a powerful weapon against Arianism. Notable among those anti-Arian bishops besides Alexander himself were Eustathius of Antioch and Marcellus of Ancyra: these two men stood in the tradition of Irenæus rather than in that of Origen. The strong Eastern supporters of the ὁμοούσιον, even with the addition of the Western bishops led by Hosius, were altogether in a minority as compared with the great body of Oriental bishops who thought like Eusebius. But with the powerful help of Constantine, only anxious for the peace of the Empire, the minority succeeded in enforcing their view upon the majority, who certainly disliked Arianism, but at the same time desired no anti-Arian novelties. As it was with Eusebius, so with the rest; when once the ὁμοούσιον had been accepted, the logical working of the Greek mind was responsible for all the other new developments, and so the Creed of Nicæa came into existence.

It must not be supposed, however, that the new creed, for all its thoroughgoing character, settled everything so as to leave no room for debate. One point is especially noteworthy. As in the theology of Origen, no distinction is made between οὐσία (essence) and ὑπόστασις (hypostasis). It was out of this identification of the two that many of the difficulties arose with which Athanasius had to deal in his defence of Nicæa. At the Council itself he was present only as deacon and attendant of Alexander; but three years afterwards, succeeding him as bishop of Alexandria, he became the central figure in the Arian controversy. Born A.D. 298, he was made bishop in 328 and died A.D. 373.

7. ATHANASIUS

The defence of the creed of Nicæa, to which Athanasius devoted his life, was made necessary because the solid front at the Council, where all but two bishops signed the creed, broke up at once in the East into the discordant parts that had only been temporarily united by the influence of the Emperor and the desire for peace. There were now three parties. There were the Arians proper, called the Anhomoians since they held that the Logos was unlike (ἀνόμοιος) to the Father. Then there were the few genuine Eastern Nicæans or Homoousians; they held to the ὁμοούσιον and had the support of the West. Finally, there was the great Oriental majority, of which Eusebius of Cæsarea is typical: these were named Homoousians, since they preferred to say that the Logos was of like essence (ὁμοιούσιος) with the Father, rather than that He was of the same essence. To them the word ὁμοούσιος remained suspect; it had a modalist or Sabellian ring, and had been condemned as used by Paul of Samosata. The majority held firmly to the three hypostases of Origen, and disliked anything that tended

H

to amalgamate them so as to destroy their individuality. They were more afraid of modalism than of inferiorism, though they did not want to be Arians. This party of the Homoiousians is commonly called Semi-Arian, but the name does not really fit.

Athanasius was prepared for the work he had to do by his own theological development before the Arian controversy. Here his *Contra Gentes* and *De Incarnatione* are most instructive. The first treatise shows him as the inheritor of the Apologetic doctrine of the Logos, only that he regards the immanence of the Logos in man not as natural but as a grace from God. By turning to lower things and consequent idolatry, man had alienated himself from the Logos; and though He was indeed manifested in the universe this was not enough. For not only was man blinded by sin, but also sin had exposed him to death, or as Athanasius says, to corruption (φθορά). The Incarnation therefore was necessary. This is explained in the second treatise as above, where Athanasius adds to the rational theology of the Apologists an interpretation of the gospel facts; but instead of following Origen, the spiritualist, he returns to Irenæus the realist.

The quintessence of his doctrine is contained in the famous sentence which gives the reasons for the Incarnation of the Logos:

'He was made man that we might be made God (Αὐτὸς γὰρ ἐπηνθρώπησεν ἵνα ἡμεῖς θεοποιηθῶμεν), and He manifested Himself by a body that we might receive the idea of the unknown Father' (*De Inc.*, 54).

These fundamental thoughts recur again and again in the later writings of Athanasius, in which he is contending against Arianism. We have noted already how he said that the Arian Logos could not deify, since He Himself was only deified by participation (*Or.*, I, 6); and that He could not communicate a true knowledge of God, since He does not truly know the Father. In a word, the Logos of Arius cannot do what is necessary to save man from the consequences of sin: the defence of Nicæa is that it proclaims an Incarnate Logos, who can both deify and reveal God.

The emphasis is above all on deification as the bestowal of incorruption (ἀφθαρσία). The revelation of God, followed by repentance on man's part, is not enough. But, says Athanasius, the law of corruption exhausted its authority in the Lord's body (*De Inc.*, 8, 4). What this means for us is made very plain in *De Sent. Dionysii*, 10, where Athanasius says:

'Just as the branches are of one essence with the vine, and are from it, so we having our bodies homogeneous with the Lord's body, receive of His fulness (Jn. i. 16), and have that body as our root for our resurrection and salvation.'

Here the conception of physical redemption is made very plain. The deviation from Origen is noteworthy. In *De Principiis*, II, 6.7, the latter says that in this life we live under the shadow of Christ, which shadow is His human soul, always exactly corresponding to the Logos. We imitate Christ's soul, as it imitates the Logos. But after this life is one beyond all shadows, which the Apostle anticipated when he said: 'Yea, though we have known Christ after the flesh, yet now we know Him so no more.' Origen spiritualizes immortality, where Athanasius conceives it realistically and regards what happens in the Lord's body as extending from it to other bodies. It is true that Athanasius, like Irenæus, also associates participation in the Spirit with deification (*De Decretis*, 3, 14). But the essence of the matter is that the Logos has deified his body, and that is the ground of the deification of others. Athanasius tersely sums up his whole case against the Arian Logos in a telling phrase: οὐκ ἂν ἐθεοποίησε θεοποιούμενος καὶ αὐτός—'He could not deify, being Himself the subject of deification' (*De Synodis*, 51). We have noted this Athanasian criticism of Arius already, when dealing with the latter.

The defence of the ὁμοούσιον against the Arians is stated more concisely in the *De Decretis* and more fully in the three famous *Orationes contra Arianos*, where the Arian proofs from Scripture are refuted at great length. (The fourth 'Oration' is not genuine.) There is a restatement of the argument in the *De Synodis* with a slight modification. It will best serve our purpose now to summarize the statement in the *De Decretis*. Here Athanasius meets the Arian argument that the name 'Son' implies a beginning of existence. He distinguishes between human and Divine generation: the one implies separation of the offspring, the other does not (IV, 20). All that he really takes from the term 'Son' at this stage is just the conception of an internal production; and when he desires to explain what this means, he passes over like Origen to the alternative names of Word and Wisdom, which he says favour the ὁμοούσιον, since Word and Wisdom properly belong to God, though inseparable from His essence (IV, 15, 20). The best images are the traditional ones of the fountain and the stream, the light and its radiance (III, 12; V, 23, 24). It is important to observe that at this point of the discussion Athanasius admits that it is the name 'Son' which creates difficulties and provokes the Arian heresy, while the names 'Word' and 'Wisdom' naturally belong to orthodoxy, providing the true exposition of the Divine Being without allowing any misconstruction (IV, 15). He goes on to say that the ὁμοούσιον was adopted by the Council to secure the unity of the Father and the Son or Logos; the Arian doctrine destroys the Divine simplicity, making the origin of the Son an accident in the Divine nature (V, 22). If it is said that the Logos had to be created for the making of other creatures, then there would be the need of a further intermediary for the creation of the Logos (III, 8). If it

is argued that ὁμοούσιον is unscriptural, much more
so are the Arian novelties anathematized at Nicæa
(III, 12). The ὁμοούσιον corresponds to the sense of
Scripture, whereas the Arian phrases do not (V, 21).
The trouble with Arianism is that it is besotted by the
word 'Inoriginate' (ἀγένητος), which comes from Greek
philosophy (VII, 28). This is not the best word by which
to begin to describe God, as it is taken from the contrast
between Him and the creatures. Prior to that is His
relation to the Son or Logos: when we pray, we pray not
to the Inoriginate, but to 'Our Father' (VII, 31).

It is clear that for Athanasius 'Father' and 'Son' are
the Divine names of religion; but, if we are to avoid
misconceptions, in theology 'Son' must be explained by
'Word' and 'Wisdom', as scripture teaches (IV, 15).
This is the position natural to Athanasius. But it is
modified somewhat in the *De Synodis* later on, where he
made concessions intended to reconcile the Homoiousians,
after a controversy with them now to be described.
Here he says that 'Son' and 'Logos' are complementary
terms: 'Logos' shows the indivisibility of the Son from the
Father, while 'Son' makes clear the hypostatic existence
of the Logos (41). Here is the germ of the further discussion which took place after his death. The discussion
was, however, already prefigured in this second great
controversy of Athanasius, this time not with the Arians
proper, but with the Homoiousian majority, who had
never been happy about the ὁμοούσιον, and who speedily
went back on it. Their suspicion that it was 'Sabellian'
seemed to be justified, when Marcellus of Ancyra, one of
its original supporters at Nicæa, developed a theology
in which he returned to Ignatius and Tertullian, thinking
of the Logos as emerging from the silence of God and the
Spirit as again proceeding from the Logos: in this way the
original Monad expanded into a Triad, until in the end
of all things by an opposite movement the Triad would

be absorbed into the Monad and God would be all in all.

The Homoiousians condemned Marcellus as a heretic at Constantinople, A.D. 336, and asserted the doctrine of the three hypostases as fundamental to the doctrine of the Trinity. Athanasius was long unwilling to part with his ancient friend and supporter; but he finally did so, and made peace with the Homoiousians, on the ground that they, though using a different language from his own, yet meant the same thing. Obedience to Scripture was what mattered. We can see the foreshadowing of this conciliatory attitude towards the Homoiousians, when even in the Orations against the Arians Athanasius continually affirms the absolute likeness in essence of Father and Son, using the word ὁμοούσιος only once in the whole long argument (I, 9). In the later *De Synodis* his position with regard to the Homoiousians is clearly stated. After attacking the Arians with the same vehemence as in his earlier works, Athanasius turns to the Homoiousians as brothers, striving to show them that they need not fear the ὁμοούσιον. In fact they themselves imply it, when they say that the Logos is both 'of the essence' and 'like in essence': to say that He is 'of the same essence' sums up both statements in one (*De Synodis*, 41).

Peace between the two parties, coupled with the entire rejection of Arianism was made at a Council held by Athanasius at Alexandria in A.D. 362. Union was established on the basis that all anti-Arians meant the same thing, and could accept the creed of Nicæa, while further denying the doctrine that the Holy Spirit was a creature and was separate from the essence of Christ (Athanasius, *Tom. ad Antiochenos*, 3). Already before the Council in his letters to Serapion Athanasius had reproved those who, while admitting the ὁμοούσιον with regard to the Son, denied it with reference to the Spirit. This view, usually associated with the name of Macedonius of

Constantinople, is fully controverted in the *Tomus ad Antiochenos*. Here Athanasius states as the common belief of all anti-Arians that there is a Holy Trinity, but only One Godhead and one Beginning; that the Son is of the same essence with the Father; and that the Holy Spirit is not a creature, but is proper to and inseparable from the essence of the Father and the Son.

The crux of the controversy between the Homoiousians and Athanasius was in the meaning to be attached to the word 'hypostasis'. It is used in the creed of Nicæa as the equivalent of οὐσία (essence). The Homoiousians, mindful of the condemnation of Paul of Samosata, feared that the ὁμοούσιον implied Modalism, 'as though the Son were non-essential or the Spirit anhypostatic' (*ib.*, 6). The Homoousian party on the other hand feared that the 'three hypostases' meant tritheism. Athanasius says that there need be no trouble about the one hypostasis or three, provided that in the former case hypostasis is understood to mean the One Essence, and in the latter to signify the Father, Son and Spirit, all truly subsisting, and yet not three Gods but only One Godhead (*ib.*, 5, 6).

In the same *Tomus ad Antiochenos* Athanasius also deals with the manner of the Incarnation. In Christ the Logos did not simply dwell as in the prophets, but was made flesh and became man, thus perfectly delivering the whole human race from sin and death. The Saviour had not a body without a soul, nor without sense and intelligence, otherwise He would not have been man, or have been the Saviour both of body and soul. But in the Incarnation the Logos is the personal element. There was not One Son of God before Abraham and another after him, but the One Son of God became man and did all the things proper to God and man (7).

8. ORTHODOX TRINITARIANISM

After Athanasius two further stages are to be recognized in the Greek doctrine of the Trinity. There is firstly a movement away from him, and then secondly a movement back towards him. The first stage denotes a partial return to Origen emphasizing the three hypostases. It is marked by the work of the three Cappadocian fathers, Basil of Cæsarea (d. A.D. 379), Gregory of Nazianzus (d. A.D. 390), and Gregory of Nyssa (d. *c.* A.D. 394). The second stage, which restores the Athanasian position belongs to John of Damascus (d. *c.* A.D. 754). Here the three hypostases are definitely subordinated to the Divine Unity by a new conception, that of their co-inherence.

The Cappadocians were moderate Origenists, belonging originally to the Homoiousian party which stood for the individual distinction of the hypostases within the One Essence. This distinction the Cappadocians continued to affirm and further to confirm by finding technical terms for its expression. The best example of their work is the Five Theological Orations of Gregory of Nazianzus, which exercised great influence on posterity. These Orations (XXVII–XXXI in the complete list of his Orations) deal with God as Trinity in Unity.

The Divine transcendence is strongly emphasized. The proper name of God is 'He that is' (ὁ ὤν), which expresses His essence better even than the name God (Θεός) [IV, 18]. The ὁμοούσιον applies equally to Father, Son and Holy Spirit. We see in the Godhead the one First Cause and the unity of rule (μοναρχία). There is a unity of essence and power (V, 14–16).

The great technical advance of the Cappadocian theology over that of Nicæa is in the separation of the terms οὐσία and ὑπόστασις. No longer are they to be used interchangeably: οὐσία applies to the Divine Unity and ὑπόστασις to the threefold distinction in the Unity. To explain what is meant Gregory says that the Divine Monarchia does not mean that God is One Person (ἓν πρόσωπον): it stands for the Trinity in which there is equality of honour as regards nature together with harmony of will and identity of efficacy. The hypostases, though not separated in essence, differ in number. The Monad from the beginning moves towards a Dyad and comes to rest in a Triad. This is what we mean when we speak of Father, Son and Holy Spirit (III, 2). The distinction is one of relation (σχέσις, III, 16). Thus expressing ourselves as well as we can in human speech, we speak of the Unbegotten (ἀγέννητον) and the Begotten (γεννητόν), while as regards the Spirit, following Jn. xv. 26, we say that He proceeds from the Father. By these three marks, 'Unbegotten,' 'Begotten' and 'Proceeding' we secure that one is called Father, another Son, and yet another Spirit, so that the distinction of the three hypostases is maintained unconfused in the one nature and dignity of the Godhead. The Three are one in the Godhead and the One is three in their properties (ἰδιότησιν) [III, 16, 17, V, 9].

This reference to the properties brings us to the philosophical distinction, borrowed from Aristotle, which Gregory uses to explain the theological distinction of the hypostases. It is that of the universal (κοινόν) and the particular (ἴδιον) [IV, 19]. In V, 11, he shows from the example of Adam, with Eve as a part of him, and Seth as their mutual progeny, how it is possible for there to be a diversity of hypostasis with unity of essence. There are three individuals, but only one human nature.

Gregory claims that his doctrine avoids the Sabellian confusion of the hypostases in one Person (πρόσωπον) and the Arian differentiation of their natures. He criticizes the ancient similes of spring, fount, river, and sun, radiance, light, as unsatisfying. He thinks it better to have done with such images, to hold fast to reverent thinking and use but few words in order to ascribe to Father, Son and Holy Spirit one Godhead and power (V, 31–33).

The undoubted effect of the Cappadocian interpretation of the Trinity, as illustrated by Nazianzen, is as might be expected from an Origenist and original Homoiousian, to emphasize the individual distinction of the hypostases till the essence becomes almost an abstraction. The use of the logical distinction of universal and particular, the illustration drawn from Adam, Eve and Seth, and the rejection of the analogies of spring, fount and river, all point towards something like Tritheism. It is, however, to be admitted that this doctrine of the individuality of the hypostases furnishes a more logical basis for the common patristic view of the Incarnation than does a doctrine which tends to resolve all distinctions into the Divine Unity. Gregory has right on his side, when he sums up the patristic doctrine of the Incarnation of the Logos in the terse form, 'What He was He remained, what He was not He assumed' (III, 19). It could not be more clearly or succinctly stated that the Logos is the personal element in the Incarnation; and this is the view of all orthodox Fathers.

It would be wrong to overlook the fact that the Cappadocians strongly denied that they taught the existence of three Gods; they stressed the unity in God as well as the distinctions, as has been already illustrated from Nazianzen's *Theological Orations*. How this stress could be actually converted into a sustained argument showing that the unity could co-exist with the distinctions, may be illustrated from Gregory of Nyssa's *Great Catechism*, chapters I and II. Here it is argued that God, like man, expresses Himself by Word (λόγος), which however being Divine is not impermanent like man's word, but is subsistent and eternal. Moreover just as our word is not altogether the same with the mind that produces it, or altogether different from it, so is it with

God and His Word. The Word of God is both the same with Him and distinct from Him.

But there is more to be said. Just as the word of man finds utterance in breath (πνεῦμα), so the Word of God finds utterance in Spirit (πνεῦμα). The difference between man's breath and God's Spirit is that the breath depends on the air external to man, whereas in God there is no dependence on anything external, so that His Spirit is an essential power with its own hypostasis, which cannot be separated either from God in Whom It is or from His Word which It accompanies.

This is a very remarkable passage, foreshadowing Augustine and Aquinas. That it had its due effect upon later Greek theology is apparent from the fact that it is taken over almost bodily by John of Damascus in his *Exposition of the Orthodox Faith*, as we shall see presently. In this connection it is fitting to mention an important term first introduced by Amphilochius of Iconium, a contemporary and friend of Basil and the two Gregories. It is the term τρόπος τῆς ὑπάρξεως, mode of existence: it is used to explain the nature of the relations constituting the hypostases. There is a very clear exposition of its meaning in Pseudo-Justin, *Expositio Rectæ Confessionis*, 3, where it is said: 'Unbegotten, Begotten and Proceeding are not names of the Essence, but are modes of existence: the mode of existence is characterized by these names; while the showing of the Essence is signified by the name of God, so that there is a difference of the Father from the Son and the Spirit according to the mode of existence, but there is identity in the matter of essence.' This work of Pseudo-Justin reflects the Nestorian controversy at the beginning of the fifth century, and is referred to by Leontius of Byzantium (A.D. 485–543); so that it belongs to the period after that of the Cappadocians, when their terminology had become common property. This termi-nology was their great legacy to posterity. It was in the

form that we have had it from Nazianzen that it maintained itself—Unbegotten, Begotten and Proceeding.
Basil and Gregory of Nyssa expressed the same meaning
in a somewhat different language which did not survive.

At a Council in Constantinople, A.D. 381, the creed of
Nicæa was reaffirmed, and the Cappadocian Trinitarianism
was sanctioned as its correct interpretation, in a document
now no longer extant. But this Council, though properly
Oriental only, was recognized by the Œcumenical Council
of Chalcedon (A.D. 451) as the second Œcumenical Council,
that of Nicæa being the first. And at Chalcedon a creed
(what is now generally known as the 'Nicene Creed')
was adopted as the creed of Nicæa confirmed and interpreted by the Council of Constantinople. Its proper name
is therefore the Niceno-Constantinopolitan creed. When
and how it originated is not known. It differs from the
original creed of Nicæa mainly in two ways. It drops the
anathemas, which were no longer suitable after οὐσία
had been distinguished from ὑπόστασις. And there is a
very considerable expansion of the article on the Holy
Spirit directed against those who denied His full Godhead.
It was now said: 'We believe in the Holy Spirit, the Lord,
the giver of life, who proceeds from the Father, who with
the Father and the Son together is worshipped and
glorified, who spoke by the prophets.'

It will be noted that it is not said that the Spirit
proceeds from the Son, as it is in the form of this creed
familiar to us as the 'Nicene Creed' of the English Prayer
Book. Greek theology regards the Father as the Beginning
and Source of the whole Godhead, as may be illustrated
from Athanasius, *Tom. ad Antiochenos*, 3, and Gregory of
Nazianzus, *Oratio de Dogmate*, 7, and *Oratio Theologica*,
III, 2.

The second and final stage in the great patristic doctrine
of the Trinity after Athanasius, which resulted in a return

to his point of view and a new emphasis on the Divine Unity, was preceded by an attempt to move in the opposite direction and to make the hypostases even more distinct than they were in the Cappadocian theology. Johannes Philoponus, Bishop of Alexandria, *c.* A.D. 550, drew the ultimate consequences of the Aristotelian logical terminology of the universal and the particular: he said that there were not only three hypostases, but also three essences, which were subsumed in the common Essence of the Godhead. This was virtually Tritheism; a tritheistic tendency was never very far away from the Cappadocian doctrine of the hypostases.

It was the work of John of Damascus, a monk of Jerusalem and the last great Greek patristic theologian (d. *c.* A.D. 754) to correct this tritheism by a renewed emphasis on the Divine Unity. He certainly follows Gregory Nazianzen more than any other previous theologian, but he does not hesitate silently to correct what he thinks wrong in him. His doctrine of God and the Trinity is contained in his *Exposition of the Orthodox Faith,* Bk. I, Chapters 1–8.

John of Damascus sums up the whole Greek doctrine of God. He is absolutely transcendent. His Essence is indeed superessential. But a knowledge of God is implanted in man by nature, and a rational proof of His existence and Unity can be drawn from the order of the creation; even a rational construction of the doctrine of the Trinity is possible. Here John practically writes out the quasi-psychological proof given in the 'Great Catechism' of Gregory of Nyssa. With this proof from the ideas of Word and Spirit Scripture agrees. There is One God, made known in three hypostases and adored with one adoration. The hypostases are one in everything but their properties of being Unbegotten, Begotten and Proceeding. The names, Fatherhood, Sonship and Procession were not applied to the Godhead by us, but were communicated to us by the Godhead. John repeats from Nazianzen the explanation of the One Godhead in three hypostases drawn from the logical distinction of the universal and the particular, and he does not hesitate even to renew the illustration from Adam, Seth and Eve, bringing out the point that Adam was unbegotten, Seth was begotten, while Eve proceeded but was not begotten. But the tendency to individualize the hypostases is corrected by the statement that the hypostases differ only in mode of subsistence (τρόπος ὑπάρξεως), and still further by the introduction of the idea of περιχώρησις, i.e. permeation or co-inherence, which has been mentioned already as John's special contribution to the doctrine of the Trinity. The hypostases are immanent in one another, though there is no confusion or mixture. Therefore, in spite of Nazianzen's cavils, John comes back to the old illustration of sun, ray and radiance, or as he more often says, fire and light; though he warns us that all analogies taken from the creatures fall short of the superessential Deity. A very remarkable passage is that in which John points out that the distinction of universal and particular applies altogether differently to God and the creatures. With the creatures we first recognize the individuals and then proceed by thought to their common essence. But with God the process is reversed. We first recognize God in His Unity, and then by thought perceive the distinctions of the hypostases.

To sum up: John of Damascus has returned in substance to the position of Athanasius on the Trinity, only that in view of subsequent discussion, the doctrine is expressed in a more precise terminology.

The study of John of Damascus brings us to the end of the Greek patristic doctrine of the Trinity. After the Council of Chalcedon the Niceno-Constantinopolitan creed was established as the one supreme Oriental confession of faith. John of Damascus represents the theological interpretation which went along with it.

There is no doubt that the final emphasis in the Greek doctrine of the Trinity is on the Unity of God. We have still to ask how far the doctrine could form the basis for an adequate Christology. It secured no doubt the Divinity of Christ; did it secure His humanity? Here we come upon a most remarkable fact. There is a hiatus between the scientific doctrine of the Trinity, which derives ultimately from the cosmic Logos philosophy of the New Testament, and the Christology accompanying it, which starts from the more concrete description of the pre-existent Son. No amount of scientific theology of the Trinity reducing the hypostases to modes of existence, substantially altered this concreteness; and the scientific Christology was formed so as to justify it. It has been recorded how Gregory Nazianzen summed up his Christological doctrine in the terse sentences: 'What He was He remained, what He was not He assumed.' It was the common agreement after the Council of Antioch that the Logos was the personal element in the historical Christ. The question therefore arose, How then could He be human?

Apollinaris of Laodicea, one of the original supporters of the homoousion at Nicæa, followed Arius so far as to say that in Christ the Logos took the place of the human mind (νοῦς). This was rejected. Gregory Nazianzen says: 'If any one puts his hope upon a mindless man, he himself lacks mind, and does not deserve complete salvation. For what is not assumed is not cured; but what is united to God is saved' [*Ep. ad Cledonium*, I, 7].

The Antiochenes Diodore and Theodore attempted to save the humanity in Christ by thinking of Him as a human person always in unity of will with the Divine Logos; but this doctrine, generally known as Nestorianism, foundered because it destroyed the unity of Christ's Person. Over against it as represented by Nestorius,

Archbishop of Constantinople, stood the victorious doctrine of Cyril, Archbishop of Alexandria, who maintained Christ to be One Hypostasis in two natures, the human nature having no hypostasis of its own. Eutyches went further and taught that the human nature was absorbed into the Divine nature of the Logos, so that there remained only one Divine-human nature. But here, at the instance of Flavian of Constantinople, Pope Leo of Rome intervened with his famous Tome, which asserted, in accordance with the old Western doctrine of Tertullian, that in the One Person of Christ the Divine and human natures remained distinct and unconfused, each operating according to its own properties. At the Council of Chalcedon (A.D. 451) the net result of the whole debate was summed up: Apollinarianism, Nestorianism and Eutychianism were rejected, and the doctrines of Cyril and Leo were combined in a formula which became henceforth the standard of orthodoxy in Christology. It was said that the two natures, Divine and human, both perfect, concurred into one Person (πρόσωπον) and one Hypostasis, 'without confusion, without alteration, without division and without separation'.

Chalcedon rejected certain interpretations of the Person of Christ, but how little it really settled is shown by the further controversies. If there were in Christ two natures and not one, were there also two wills and two energies, or did the unity of the Person require that there should be only one will and one unity of operation? Rome, still following the line of Tertullian and Leo, stood for two wills and two energies, and the sixth Œcumenical Council, held at Constantinople in A.D. 681, confirmed the Roman doctrine.

In the end, however, Greek theology, accepting the two wills and the two energies, found the way to interpret them so as once more to emphasize the unity of Christ's Person. It was again John of Damascus who came to the

rescue. Already in the sixth century Leontius of
Byzantium had put forward the doctrine of *enhypostasis*.
The human nature of Christ, he said, though not itself a
hypostasis, was nevertheless not without hypostasis
(ἀνυπόστατος). It was *enhypostatic* (ἐνυπόστατος), having
its hypostasis in the Logos. Adopting this doctrine, John
of Damascus went on to make use of the same principle
that he had used in the doctrine of the Trinity, that of
permeation (περιχώρησις). Though the natures remain
distinct, each shares in the properties of the other. Not
just an interchange of names is meant after the manner
of Tertullian, but rather a real communication of properties. The exchange, however, is one-sided. The impassible Divine nature does not share in the sufferings
of the human nature; but the human nature is deified
and becomes omniscient. Moreover, though there is a
human will, there is no human choice (προαίρεσις)
[*Exposition of the Orthodox Faith*, Bk. III, esp. 13, 16, 19].
It is clear that the Greek doctrine shies away once more
from admitting anything resembling the full humanity
of Christ.

9. AUGUSTINE

The Greek patristic doctrines of the Trinity and the
Incarnation come to an end with John of Damascus.
But we must now go back in time to a highly original
and largely independent treatment of the doctrine of the
Trinity in Latin theology. Augustine has left a great work,
De Trinitate, written over many years A.D. 400–418.
He writes after the settlement of the Arian controversy,
and after Hilary (d. 367) and Ambrose (d. 397) had
familiarized the West with the Greek anti-Arian theology.
Augustine, however, was not at home in Greek, and was
not satisfied with what he found in Latin. Moreover, he
had a different soteriology from that of the Greeks.
Harnack has called him 'the reformer of Christian piety'.

I

What this means needs explanation, if we are to understand Augustine on the Trinity.

Whatever more the Incarnation was conceived to have done for human salvation, it was held in the Christian Church from the second century onwards to have revealed afresh God, His law, and the promise of immortality. As Athanasius puts it in *De Incarnatione*, 16, it was intended to accomplish two works of Divine love. One was the communication of immortality to human nature, the other was the manifestation of the way by which the gift could be secured by the individual. This way was that of obedience to the Divine law after the forgiveness of sins had been received in baptism.

In the West Tertullian sharpened what was the common belief of all Christians about obedience into a precise doctrine of merit and reward, which included a doctrine of satisfaction for postbaptismal sin by means of supererogatory merit. It was in this form that the whole doctrine came down to Augustine. He found the position altogether unsatisfactory. His own experience was that without the grace of God man could not obey the law and merit salvation. He declared: 'When God crowns our merits, He crowns His own gifts' (*Ep.*, 194, 5, 19). Therefore his prayer was: 'Grant what Thou commandest, and command what Thou wilt' [*Conf.*, X, 29, 40]. It was in thus emphasizing the grace of God that Augustine became the reformer of Christian piety. A new spirit breathes in his writings. It is only right to recognize that it depends in part on his schooling in Neoplatonism, yet it depends even more on the Bible and in particular on the Book of Psalms. Thus if on the one hand his thought expressed itself in the words, 'I desire to know God and the soul. Nothing more. Nothing at all' [*Soliloq.*, I, 2, 7]; on the other hand nothing better expressed his religion than the Psalmist's cry, 'Say unto my soul, I am thy salvation' [Ps. xxxv.; 3 *Conf.*, I, 5, 5].

It is the combination of acute reasoning with the spirit of devotion that marks Augustine's great work on the Trinity. He accepted the doctrine on the authority of Scripture and the Church, and desired to understand it as far as possible. It is no wonder that a man of his temper should stress the Divine Unity even more than any of the theologians previously studied. He is immensely emphatic on the point. The Trinity is One God, and the distinction of the Persons does not destroy the Divine Simplicity, in which all the Divine attributes are one with the Divine Essence (*De Trin.*, XV, 5, 8). The operation of the Trinity in the world is inseparable. The Trinity operates as One God and One Creator (IV, 21, 30). This Unity of God is expressed by saying that He is One Substance. Nevertheless in the Unity there are three Persons. This is the doctrine of Scripture, as Augustine shows in detail. Moreover Scripture teaches the absolute equality of the Persons, as is shown at length in Bks. I and II. Here Augustine differs from the Greek doctrine, according to which the Father is the Source of the whole Godhead (πηγὴ Θεότητος). The Father and the Son are equally the origin (*principium*) of the Spirit (V. 14, 15). Augustine found the key to the distinction of the Persons in a conception which we have found already in Nazianzen, that of relation (σχέσις, *relativum*). Father, Son and Spirit are distinguished only by their mutual relations.

As regards terminology, Augustine uses the traditional Western language in speaking of One Substance and Three Persons. He decides against the alternative terminology of One Essence and Three Substances, which would be the literal equivalent of the Greek μία οὐσία, τρεῖς ὑποστάσεις. He thinks 'three Persons' more convenient (*commodius*) than 'three Substances' (VII, 5, 10). But even the word 'person' does not satisfy him. We say 'three Persons', not as though that meant really saying something worth while, but simply so as not to say nothing at all (V, 9, 10). The mystery is beyond human language.

Nevertheless, Augustine's inquiring and speculative mind sought to understand the mystery. The really novel thing in his *De Trinitate* is the immense labour that he has taken to find an analogy to the Trinitarian life of God in the working of the human mind. He uses different forms of the analogy, but the most important in view of its future development by Aquinas is that of the mind, the knowledge that it has of itself, and the love by which it loves itself (XV, 6, 10). Just so, God is a Spirit that knows Himself and loves Himself as known. But Augustine warns us that all analogies taken from the human mind fall short (XV, 27, 49).

In VI, 6, 11 Augustine says that we do not call the three Persons One Person, but rather One God and One Essence. But all the same, with his psychological analogy, he has gone a long way towards thinking of God in 'personal terms', where these stand not just for the three hypostases of the Trinity but for the whole Trinity itself conceived as the Living God of the Old Testament. We may admit that it is only analogically that God is so thought of: the Greeks were right in saying that all our conceptions of God are anthropomorphic: what else could they be? And we may further admit that Augustine is right in saying therefore that our best analogies fall short. But the point is that he has found the best analogy, and so more than any other theologian of the ancient Church has effectively united the Christian doctrine of the Trinity with the Old Testament emphasis on the Divine Unity.

It has been said repeatedly that the Greek doctrine of the Incarnation does not sufficiently recognize the humanity of Christ. Hilary, who brought over the West to accept the Greek Trinitarianism, in his *De Trinitate* carried the principle that the Logos is the personal element in Christ to the point of docetism. He only ate and drank as a concession to our habits, not from necessity (X, 24). His body was capable of suffering, but he could not feel grief (X, 35). But this was altogether an eccentricity in Western theology. The much more influential Augustine however also accepts the doctrine that the Logos is the personal element in Christ. He found an analogy for the Person of Christ in the constitution of man: 'As man is one person, the rational soul and the flesh, so Christ is One Person, the Word and the man' (*Serm.*, CLXXIV, 2). He also taught that human nature in no way merited assumption into the Divine Person. He saw in the Incarnation the supreme example of the same grace by which man is saved (*Euch.*, 36). We note that in this last statement there is some tendency to assimilate Christ with other men: there is even greater emphasis on His humanity in other places. Augustine says in *Conf.*, X, 43, 68: 'So far as He is man, so far is He Mediator.' And again in *De Civ. Dei*, IX, 15, 2, even more forcibly: 'Not yet is He Mediator in that He is the Word . . . but He is Mediator in virtue of His being man.'

To complete the account of the patristic doctrine of the Trinity and to keep an eye on that of the Incarnation, three more things are necessary. Firstly, notice must be taken of the 'Athanasian' Creed. Secondly, something must be said of Spanish Adoptianism. And, thirdly, we have to note the separation of the Eastern and Western Churches over the addition of the '*filioque*' in the Niceno-Constantinopolitan Creed.

The 'Athanasian' Creed (which has nothing to do with Athanasius) originated in Gaul in the fifth or sixth century A.D., being mainly taken from Augustine's teaching on the Trinity and the Incarnation. What it sets out, however, is his apprehension of the Scriptural data rather than his attempt to understand them. It is said that the Catholic faith is to worship One God in Trinity, neither confounding the Persons, nor dividing the Substance. The Three Persons are distinct from one another, co-equal and co-eternal; but their Godhead is One. Each Person is God, yet there are not three Gods, but only One God. The Father is of none, the Son of the Father only, the Holy Ghost is of the Father and the Son. In the Incarnation Jesus Christ, the Son of God is Perfect God and Perfect Man, yet not two, but one Christ, by taking of the manhood into God. Augustine's illustration is used: as the reasonable soul and flesh is one man, so God and man is one Christ.

The East has never used this symbol. As has been noticed already, its sole standard of faith is the Niceno-Constantinopolitan Creed. The Athanasian Creed came into general use in the West from the ninth century onwards. Besides subscribing to the Niceno-Constantino-politan Creed together with the East, the West also continued to cherish the 'Apostles' Creed i.e. the Roman baptismal confession, which assumed somewhat varying forms, until from the time of Charlemagne onwards it came to be fixed in its present state. In the Middle Ages the West recognized all three creeds, the 'Apostles', the 'Nicene' and the 'Athanasian'. But from the sixth century onwards the 'Nicene' Creed was used with the addition of the *filioque*, ascribing the procession of the Holy Spirit not only to the Father but also to the Son as source. Of this more anon.

Meanwhile, a glance at Christology. One more attempt to give independent substance to Christ's humanity was made in Spanish Adoptianism. This arose within the Augustinian tradition which ruled in Spain. Augustine had spoken of the assumption of human nature by the Logos as an act of pure grace, and both he and other Latin fathers at times had varied the phrase by speaking of the assumption of a man, a form of words not even unknown to the Greeks. Occasionally, moreover, the

Latins had varied *homo assumptus* with *homo adoptivus*, and the phrase had found its way into the Spanish liturgy. Elipandus, Archbishop of Toledo, therefore in A.D. 785 felt no difficulty in interpreting the creed of Chalcedon to mean that as far as His human nature was concerned, Christ was the adopted Son of God entirely like other men, sin except. But this doctrine was vehemently repudiated by the Frankish theologians of Charlemagne's empire, amongst whom Alcuin was prominent. He said that in the assumption of the flesh by God, the person disappears, leaving only the nature. Adoptianism was condemned at one council after another before the end of the century. The result was that the doctrine of *enhypostasis* became the one and only interpretation of the Person of Christ in the West as well as in the East.

Yet the Frankish theologians were not subservient to Eastern orthodoxy in all things. The introduction of the '*filioque*' into the 'Nicene' Creed in the West was also begun in the time of Charlemagne, and was defended against the Greeks by his theologians. Rome approved the doctrine, and somewhat later in A.D. 1014 began to use the creed in the Mass with the '*filioque*' addition. East and West now stood divided on the point.

III.—ASSIMILATION, CRITICISM AND RECONSTRUCTION

1. AQUINAS

OUR study of the doctrine of the Trinity may now be said to be complete so far as the orthodox doctrine with the accompanying Christology is concerned. Except for the disagreement over the *filioque*, both the doctrines of the Trinity and the Incarnation were settled for the churches which accepted as their standard of belief, either the 'Nicene' Creed alone, or along with the 'Apostles' and the 'Athanasian' Creeds. The former applies of course to the Greek Orthodox Church; the latter not only to the Roman Catholic Church, but also to the great Lutheran and Reformed Protestant Churches on the Continent as well as to the Church of England, and the Church of Scotland. The substance of the Creeds was also accepted by English Protestant Dissent, even when they were not formally recognized. But the meaning of the doctrines of the Trinity and the Incarnation has been different in the various churches, even when the same doctrines have been accepted.

It has been explained already how these doctrines form the essential soteriology of the Greeks. It is worthwhile on this point to quote Gregory Nazianzen to show how subordinate in his mind were many other things apart from the Trinity and the Incarnation, which other ages and Church-systems different from his have thought most important. He says in *Orat.*, XXVII, 10 (1st Theological): 'You may philosophize about the world and the

worlds, about matter, about the soul, about reasonable
natures better and worse, about resurrection, judgment,
retribution, and the sufferings of Christ, for in these
matters success is not unprofitable and failure is harmless.'

In the later theology of the Greek Orthodox Church
from John of Damascus onwards there was a widening of
the field to take in much of what Nazianzen considered
unimportant. But the Dogma of the Incarnation with
that of the Trinity as its presupposition continued to be
the dogma *par excellence*; though the doctrine of physical
redemption fell into the background, and instead the
Incarnation came to be explained as the way in which
the guilt of sin was removed and final beatitude was
assured.

In Roman Catholicism there has been a still greater
shifting of interest. True, the doctrine of the Incarnation,
supported by that of the Trinity has maintained its
place as the basis of all other doctrinal superstructure.
But the Western Church in the Middle Ages, building its
doctrine by the principles of authority and reason, had a
new outlook. Authority certainly meant, firstly Scripture,
and then the Fathers in general; but in reality Augustine
towered over the rest of the Fathers and prescribed the
interpretation of Scripture. Thus it was that a new stress
fell upon the humanity of Christ, even though only the
doctrine of *enhypostasis* was orthodox. According to
Anselm's *Cur Deus Homo* (he died A.D. 1109) Christ
made satisfaction for human sin and merited salvation
for men as Himself man, while His Godhead came in to
give an infinite value to His work. In the theological
system of St. Thomas Aquinas, the crowning work of
Medieval theology, and still the standard of Roman
belief, Anselm's theory is converted into the doctrine that
Christ made satisfaction for sin and merited for men the
grace by which they in turn can merit salvation. In this
way the Incarnation received its classical Medieval

meaning along the lines of Augustine's theology. Abelard's alternative interpretation of it, also derived from Augustine, should not be forgotten: it was a revelation of God's love, kindling a responsive love to God.

The doctrine of the Trinity, however, continued to be fundamental as the ground of everything else, and great labour was spent upon it by the Medieval theologians, with whom from the eleventh century onwards reason came to be identified more and more with the Aristotelian philosophy. The old antitheses naturally came to life again. Roscellin was condemned at Soissons in A.D. 1092 for tritheism; as a nominalist in philosophy he held the Essence to be only a common name for the three individual Persons. Abelard on the other hand, who explained the Persons as embodying God's Power, Wisdom and Love, was condemned at the same place in 1121, being charged with Modalism; his enemies said that his doctrine was not the distinction, but the destruction of the Persons. The only really new development in the doctrine of the Trinity came from Boethius (d. A.D. 525), Richard of St. Victor (d. A.D. 1173) and Thomas Aquinas (d. A.D. 1274).

Boethius is notable as the first to begin the translation of Aristotle into Latin; he is also specially important for our subject in virtue of the Aristotelian definition which he gave of the term 'person': '*persona est naturæ rationalis individua substantia*'—a person is an individual substance of a rational nature. This definition was utilized in the Middle Ages both for Christology and for the doctrine of the Trinity. It fitted in well with the dominant Christology, but was more difficult to apply in the doctrine of the Trinity, where this followed Augustine.

Richard is noteworthy for two things. He sought to fit the definition to the Trinity, suggesting '*divinæ naturæ incommunicabilis existentia*'—an incommunicable existence of the Divine nature. He also anticipated the social doctrine of the Trinity which has been much to the fore in recent times. The following account of his social Trinitarianism is summarized from his work, *De Trinitate*, III, 1-25: The existence of a Trinity in God can be proved by reason, since God is Absolute Love conjoined with Absolute Power and Absolute Beatitude. One Person alone in God is insufficient. He must have a Second Person as the worthy object of His love. But even the two Persons are insufficient: they must desire a third to share the bliss of their mutual love and so complete their beatitude. Since, however, God is Absolute Power, He can do everything necessary for His complete satisfaction, and so God's Absolute Love and Absolute Beatitude result in the three Persons of the Trinity.

Thomas Aquinas, the greatest theologian of the Middle Ages, has given in his *Summa Theologica* a classical statement of the doctrine of the Trinity which systematizes and supplements Augustine. It is contained in *Summa*, I, qu. 27-43. For the proper understanding of the Thomist doctrine it is important to observe that it is set in the framework of a great doctrine of God and His attributes, which occupies I, qu. 2-26.

God is known to us by natural reason as the First Cause of the Universe. But when we ask What He is, we can only answer in negative terms. He is in every way Infinite. It can however be said without any contradiction of His infinity that He is altogether Simple, and is absolutely Perfect and One. All His attributes are one and the same with His Essence. We can only name Him by means of analogies drawn from the creatures. But thereby the way is opened for the Biblical description of God as Intelligence and Will, and as Love, Righteousness, Mercy and Power, in fact as a Living God.

The doctrine of the Trinity, however, cannot be proved by natural reason; it depends upon revelation, as given in Scripture (qu. 32, art. 1). Any analogies that may be used to explain it are insufficient to prove it. For explanation, however, they are useful. Thus we may say that there is process within God in two ways (qu. 27). The Divine Intellect, which is One with the Divine Essence, produces an Image of itself, which being Divine is consubstantial and co-equal with Itself. Thus is explained the Father's begetting of the Son. But upon this first internal process in God there follows a second, which is that of the Divine Will (also one with the Divine Essence), directed towards the Image conceived by the Intellect. This process is not a begetting as in the former case: its result is Love, which being a living impulse is properly called Spirit. As the process is not begetting, it has no special name, but may be called 'breathing' (*spiratio*). The result of the process, being again Divine, is consubstantial and co-equal with the Father and the Son.

The Persons of the Trinity are thus constituted by the internal relations of the Divine Essence, which are those of generation and procession (or spiration). Apart from these relations there is only the One Divine Essence (qu. 28). But what are the Persons so constituted? It must first be noted that the relations are real, whereas the distinction of the Divine attributes from one another is rational only: there are no real distinctions in God except so far as there are opposed relations of origin. Thomas discusses the Persons in accordance with this general point of view (qu. 29). He begins with the definition of Boethius, 'A person is an individual substance of a rational nature'; he says that the synonyms of 'person' are 'subsistence' (*subsistentia*) and 'hypostasis'. The natural Latin equivalent for the Greek 'hypostasis' would be 'substance'; but it is best avoided in this connection, because it is equivocal, as it can also stand for the Divine Essence. The definition of Boethius is very well, but an important caution is now added. Since all names used of God are used only in a higher sense, it is so with the names 'person' and 'hypostasis'. Their use is limited by their subject-matter. Still they have their uses. Though they are not found in Scripture, any more than the name Trinity, they are used to express what is certainly there implied. They bring out the meaning in opposition to heresy.

It is very noteworthy that Thomas, whether he is using the Scriptural terms Father, Son, and Spirit, or is speaking of the Persons of the Trinity, always goes back to his original doctrine of the double procession of Intellect and Will in God when he comes to explain either what Scripture or ecclesiastical tradition mean. The doctrine of the double procession is his real doctrine of the Trinity: it is of course a systematization and restatement of the original ideas of Augustine. But attention was called earlier to the fact that Athanasius like other Greek Fathers, when he desires to explain Father and Son turns naturally to the alternatives of God and His Wisdom or Logos, and explains 'generation' thereby. We see in Aquinas the culmination of a process of thought, which goes back to Greek theology, becomes more definite in Augustine, and now is raised to absolute clarity of meaning. This meaning is that so far as the inner life of God is to be understood by men, the truest analogies are those of psychology. Cp. I Cor. ii. 11.

In this connection it is important to observe that Thomas, while approving Richard of St. Victor's new definition of Person as 'an incommunicable existence of the Divine nature' (qu. 28, art. 3 ad 4), disallows the social analogy suggested by him for the Trinity. He says that it proceeds by an analogy with human society, where there can only be joyous possession of good in fellowship. But God who has all good in Himself needs no fellow. Therefore the analogy is inapplicable (I, 32, 1 ad 2).

It goes without saying that in spite of his quasi-modalist doctrine of the Trinity, Aquinas is still faithful to the doctrine of *enhypostasis*, when he treats of the Incarnation.

The Divine and human natures are united in the Divine hypostasis of the Word (*S. Theol.*, III, qu. 2, art. 3), i.e., in Christ the Divine Son of God is the subject, while the humanity is a predicate. After the condemnation of Spanish adoptianism no other position was possible to a medieval theologian. Nevertheless, the Thomist doctrine of the Trinity is a landmark in the history of our subject, setting a pattern for the future development of the doctrine. Moreover, on the whole it is singularly free from what Thomas himself recognized as the besetting sin of Medieval Scholasticism, 'the multiplication of useless questions, articles and arguments' (*S. Theol.*, I, Prologus).

It was this proliferation of syllogistic argument in the later scholasticism of Duns Scotus and Ockham that provoked the revolt from it which marks the simple piety as well as the mysticism of the later Middle Ages. Typical of this revolt is the salient passage previously quoted from Thomas à Kempis:—'What will it avail thee to argue profoundly of the Trinity, if thou be void of humility and art thereby displeasing to the Trinity?' No slight is intended to the doctrine of the Trinity, but objection is taken to the substitution of scholastic argument for personal religion. It is the same thought as that of the *Theologia Germanica* (Chapter XIX), which says that we cannot come to the Christ-life 'by much questioning, or by hearsay, or by reading and study, nor yet by high skill and great learning'. Only by the renunciation of self and the world is it possible.

2. RENAISSANCE AND REFORMATION

A still more potent antagonism to the subtleties of the scholastic theology resulted from the Renaissance of the late fifteenth century. Though it started as a renewed study of the pagan classics, it exercised a powerful influence upon theology when its methods were applied to the Christian classics, the Fathers and the Scriptures, especially the New Testament. The representative man here is Erasmus (d. 1536). He did not deny the value of the scholastic theology in the hands of the learned, but he aimed at satisfying the needs of the laity by means of a Christian philosophy, concerned not with speculation on the Divine essence, but with the recognition of God's operation in the world, and with the teaching and example of Jesus Christ. Thus by a very different route he reached the same position as that of à Kempis, whose theme also was the imitation of Christ. A particularly important part of the work of Erasmus was his editing of the Greek New Testament. It was a landmark in the history of Trinitarianism when he left out I Jn. v. 7 as spurious, even though in a later edition under pressure he reinserted the verse.

The doctrine of the Reformation also began as a revolt from the scholastic theology. Certainly Luther, Zwingli, Melanchthon, and Calvin were all strictly orthodox both as to the doctrine of the Trinity and as to that of the Incarnation. It has been mentioned already that the great Lutheran and Reformed churches maintained the same position. This is shown for Lutheranism by the Augsburg Confession of 1531 and 1540; for the various Reformed churches, including the Church of Scotland, by the Helvetic Confession of 1536, the Belgic Confession of 1561 and the Westminster Confession 1647.

Yet there was a new spirit moving in the Reformation, and at first it almost seemed as if there might be a complete transformation of the theological system. Luther's doctrine of justification by faith was the focus of the new point of view. Aquinas, representing medieval theology in general, and interpreting Augustine, had said that infused grace was a quality of the soul, which as received by the sinner made him actually just, the forgiveness of sins accompanying the change. But Luther, going back to Paul, taught that grace was the free favour of God, while justification was God's accounting of the sinner righteous and forgiving his sins. Luther further taught that the sole condition of such justification was trust in God as revealed in Christ: this trust or confidence was saving faith. Here too was a difference from Aquinas and the medieval theology. From the days of the Ancient Church faith had always meant belief in the creed as summarizing Scripture. Aquinas taught that to be true and saving faith belief must be informed by love, resulting from infused grace. Thus for Luther both grace and faith came to have new meanings, as compared with those stated by Aquinas. It was indeed a theological revolution. What was to follow from it? It is to be noted that Luther and the other Reformers, and Protestants in general, still presupposed simple belief, when they added to it confidence or trust to disclose the whole meaning of faith.

The first result of the new point of view was the fixing upon Scripture as the one and only primary authority in matters of belief. Paul, not Augustine, was to be followed on justification, grace and faith. If the ancient creeds still stood, it was because they truly expressed the sense of Scripture. There was something else that agreed with Scripture, that was the experience of the Christian; to this then also Luther appealed as the testimony of the Holy Spirit. Calvin followed him; but he makes it clear in the *Institutes* that experience does but confirm Scripture. Still the third principle in theology besides authority and reason had now been given a place: in future days it was to come to its own.

As regards reason, Luther as a fully trained theologian, used logical argument with great vigour; but reason was for him no independent source of religious truth. Speculative theory on God's essence he called '*theologia gloriæ*' and cared nothing for it. God was to be sought in the humanity of Christ. The true Christian theology was a '*theologia crucis*', whose subject was the justification of the sinner. Luther accordingly utilized both the ancient doctrines of the Trinity and the Incarnation, and the medieval doctrines of Christ's satisfaction and merit, the latter considerably changed to suit his new point of view; but he used them in no systematic way, but always through them to set forth his own doctrine of grace and faith.

It is no wonder, therefore, that when the first attempts were made to systematize Protestant theology, the new doctrine should drive the doctrines of the Trinity and the Incarnation into the background. Well known are the words of Melanchthon in the Introduction to the first edition of his *Loci Theologici* (A.D. 1521):—'To know Christ is to know His benefits, not as the Schoolmen teach, to know His natures and the modes of His incarnation.' But Melanchthon goes even further in the same context, saying: 'There is no reason why we should spend much labour over those supreme topics of God, His Unity and Trinity, the mysteries of creation and the modes of the Incarnation. I ask you, what the scholastic theologians have achieved in so many ages by occupying themselves with these questions alone?'

Calvin also in the first edition of his *Institutio* (A.D. 1536) gave comparatively little space to the Trinity and the Incarnation. In the end, because of the need of complete systematic instruction, both subjects receive a sufficiently full treatment in Melanchthon's *Loci* of 1535 and Calvin's *Institutio* of 1559. The latter work is acknowledged to be the masterpiece of Protestant theology. Reason is here recognized in that a natural knowledge of God is admitted; but because this knowledge has been made ineffective by man's sin, the revelation in Scripture is necessary. Calvin proposes the *Institutio* as a key to

K

Scripture, arranging its topics in due order. As has been mentioned already, the testimony of the Holy Spirit is brought in to confirm Scripture, but it is given no real control in the formation of doctrine.

The constant triad of authority, reason and experience governed the whole great doctrinal development in the seventeenth century. Scripture was basal; reason was used instrumentally to draw out its meaning, constructively to provide a natural theology, and destructively to overthrow heresy. Experience was still a theological Cinderella, whose time of triumph was not yet.

Calvin says that God is One and is Infinite, but that He designates Himself as existing in three Persons in order to give us a more intimate knowledge of His nature. Otherwise our knowledge of Him would be bare and empty. The doctrine of the Trinity which follows is full, but without the minutiæ of scholastic discussion. It is Scriptural and patristic rather than scholastic—the same is true of Melanchthon's doctrine of A.D. 1535. But the seventeenth century saw the birth of great scholastic systems, both Lutheran and Reformed, where the doctrines of the Trinity and the Incarnation were treated with all the subtlety and detail which they had enjoyed in the Middle Ages. Old controversies were renewed. Lutheran theologians accused Reformed theologians of Sabellianism, because they showed a dislike of the term 'person', preferring 'hypostasis', or still better τρόπος ὑπάρξεως, mode of subsistence. There was also a controversy in the doctrine of the Incarnation over the *communicatio idiomatum*. The Lutheran watchword was '*finitum capax infiniti*'; that of the Reformed was '*finitum non capax infiniti*'. The former taught like John of Damascus that Christ's human nature shared in every operation of His Divinity, the latter maintained that it had no part in the cosmic work of the Logos. Because, like Leo of Rome, the Reformed insisted on the permanent distinction of the natures, the Lutherans charged them with Nestorianism. It is observable that the Reformed tendency to modalism in the doctrine of the Trinity accompanies their interest in the humanity of Christ. The two naturally go together.

But the Lutherans had to provide for the manifestation of humanity in the gospel story of Jesus. As their doctrine of the Incarnation required a complete deification of His humanity, they referred to Phil. ii. 5–11 and taught a doctrine of *Kenosis*, so that in Christ's earthly life there was a restraint of His Divinity, even though it was so intimately conjoined to His humanity. Some Lutherans, however, refused to go as far as this; they taught that there was simply a *krypsis*, or hiding of Christ's Divine attributes in His life on earth.

A word must now be added on the parallel development of theology in England. Here, because of the special circumstances of the English Reformation, theological debate was centred on polity rather than on doctrine as such. The greatest English theological work of the sixteenth century is Hooker's treatise, *Of the Laws of Ecclesiastical Polity*, which defends the constitution of the Church of England against Puritan objections. Incidentally, however, Hooker states the orthodox doctrines of the Trinity and the Incarnation in a form that has become classic for later Anglicanism (*op. cit.*, V, 51–54). The Church of England was of course committed to these doctrines in their patristic form by its use of the three creeds, Apostles', Nicene, and Athanasian in its services. But, before leaving the subject of post-Reformation theology in England, it is worthwhile to refer to the Savoy Declaration, issued in 1658 by the Independents. Saying that all decrees of Councils and Opinions of ancient writers are to be examined and judged by Scripture as alone finally authoritative, they yet say that the doctrine of the Trinity 'is the foundation of all our Communion with God, and comfortable Dependence upon Him'. No words could better illustrate the way in which Orthodox Dissent, as well as Anglicanism stood towards Trinitarianism.

3. ANTI-TRINITARIANISM

We have now to turn to a very different subject from that which has engaged us up to the present. It is Anti-Trinitarianism. No longer is the theme that of disputes about the Trinity and the Incarnation, but rather the absolute denial of the orthodox doctrines considered by Greek Orthodox, Catholics and Protestants to be firmly established on the basis of Scripture. We have seen the aversion of simple piety in the later Middle Ages from the scholastic subtleties introduced into these doctrines; we have noted a similar aversion in the learned humanist, Erasmus, and have observed the evidence of a similar feeling in the early work of Melanchthon and Calvin. But now we have to chronicle not only aversion, but also entire objection and attempted refutation. It is easy to understand how aversion prepared the way for denial, which followed upon it when the Reformation principle of the sole authority of Scripture was used in criticism, not only of the Medieval doctrines of grace, faith and justification, but even of the doctrines of the Trinity and the Incarnation, hitherto regarded as fundamental and sacrosanct. To the service of this criticism were adapted by its principal exponent both the humanist scholarship of the Renaissance descending from Erasmus, and the subtlety of logical argument that marked the later Medieval scholasticism. This supreme exponent of Anti-Trinitarianism was Faustus Socinus (d. 1604). Before him there were others, notably Servetus (d. 1553), remembered for his fatal clash with Calvin. But it was Socinus who cut his name deeply into the history of theology as

the great protagonist of Anti-Trinitarianism, who gave
infinite trouble to his orthodox opponents, and who
started a movement the results of which are felt to this
day.

Socinus maintained that Scripture, which was still for
him the supreme authority, was to be interpreted, not
by the ancient creeds, but by reason. His own reason,
working upon Scripture produced results very different
from the credal statements. His anti-Trinitarianism is
summarized in the Racovian Catechism, published after
his death (qu. 21–23). Here it is said that the Essence
of God is only One Person. The proof is, 'because the
Divine Essence is single only in number, and therefore
there cannot be several persons in it. For a person is
nothing else than an intelligent, indivisible essence'.
This single Divine Person is the One God, the Father of
Our Lord Jesus Christ. For proof the Catechism quotes
Jn. xvii. 3, I Cor. viii. 6 and Eph. iv. 6, all asserting the
Unity of God. It is to be noted that it uses what is virtually
the Boethian definition of 'person' to destroy the idea of a
Trinity of Persons in God.

To appreciate to the full the Socinian innovation
we may recall Nazianzen's assertion that the Divine
Monarchia does not mean that God is One Person (ἓν
πρόσωπον), but stands for the Trinity. In orthodox Greek
theology God's Unity was always represented by οὐσία
(essence); but here Socinianism boldly equates 'essence'
with 'person'. Augustine and Aquinas, going beyond
Greek beginnings in the same direction had combined the
thought of God's transcendent infinity with psychological
analogies for the Trinity; but they had not ventured to
call God a 'Person'—His Unity was still represented by
'Essence' or 'Substance'. It has been said that Socinus has
left a deep mark on the history of Christian theology.
Though we shall have presently to observe an exception
to the rule, modern theology in general has accepted the

thought of God as a 'Person': this is where Socinus has cut deepest, and his influence has been most permanent. Of course the idea of personality has been immeasurably deepened since the days of Socinus, notably by the concept of self-consciousness. The application of this concept to God is indeed already virtually present in the doctrine of Augustine and Aquinas. But in modern theology in general 'person' and self-consciousness completely unite; and the great problem becomes how to join both with the idea of infinity, when they are applied to God. The best that has been done for the solution of the problem is to be found in Lotze's *Microcosmus* (Bk. IX, Chapter 4).

The Christology of Socinianism was frankly adoptianist. Christ, though miraculously born of a virgin, is a man who is our teacher, law-giver and example. That He made satisfaction for sin was strongly denied; He only proclaimed the Divine forgiveness. But it was taught that He rose from the dead, and that God exalted Him to rule in His kingdom as His representative.

The teaching on the Holy Spirit is the natural accompaniment of the adoptianist Christology. No more than Christ is the Holy Spirit a Divine Person. In the article '*De cognitione Dei*' of his *Christianæ Religionis Institutio*, Socinus says that the Spirit is simply a certain power and efficacy of God Himself, as is indeed suggested by the literal meaning of the word 'spirit', which is 'breath'.

As Socinus and the Socinians accepted Scripture as supernatural revelation, they had the task of showing its agreement with their doctrine. In so doing they utilized the Renaissance scholarship, and exhibited much acumen. The affinity of Socinianism with the original Messianic *kerygma* is sufficiently evident; though it must be added that the Socinians rationalized the *kerygma* by refusing to admit that it pointed beyond itself in its assimilation of Jesus with the JAHWEH of the Old Testament. Still,

Socinianism must be regarded as yet another revolt of the original *kerygma* against the Pauline and Johannine theologies. The Racovian Catechism indeed attempts to explain away the doctrine of Christ's pre-existence, when it interprets Paul and John, but it is driven to very forced expedients. Some Socinian theologians compromised by admitting an ideal pre-existence of Christ.

Socinianism produced an immense ferment within the Protestant churches. Orthodox Protestantism of course could only oppose it. But in Holland, where the humanism of Erasmus still worked on, Arminius had broken away from orthodoxy on the subject of predestination. He died in 1609, but Arminianism grew and throve, producing a complete theological system of its own, which was characterized by a spirit of reasonableness altogether opposed to the authoritarianism of orthodoxy. It was therefore naturally more open to Socinian influence. The result was that while the Arminian theologians did not deny the doctrine of the Trinity, they proposed to dispense with all the technical terms which went beyond what was found in Scripture. This form of thought was quite as offensive to the orthodox as the overt Anti-trinitarianism of Socinus, but it was much more insidious in its influence. Nowhere was this influence more remarkable than in England. It produced in an important school of Anglican theologians an anti-dogmatic temper and a desire to concentrate on the essentials of religion only. These were the Latitudinarians of the second half of the seventeenth century, who while remaining in conformity with the Church of England and loving its liturgy, sought a refuge from the controversies of the time in a Neoplatonic mysticism.

A still more radical exercise of the spirit of reason was the English Deism. If the Latitudinarians had returned practically to the standpoint of Clement of Alexandria who found the essence of Christianity in a mystical Gnosis, the Deists went back still further and renewed the position of the second century Apologists, according to which the Christian religion was in substance the knowledge of God, the moral law and the promise of immortality. Lord Herbert of Cherbury, the father of Deism, summed it up in five points [*De Veritate*, 1624]: (1) There is a Supreme Being; (2) He is to be worshipped; (3) Piety and virtue are the chief elements in His worship; (4) Sin is to be expiated by repentance and amendment; (5) There are Divine rewards and punishments after death. Attaching himself to the Stoic philosophy Lord Herbert claimed that these points of doctrine were to be found as 'common notions' in the mind of every man. They are, as will be seen, equivalent to what the Apologists attributed to the instruction of the Logos immanent in the mind, with the addition of the necessity of repentance which derives from the Christian *kerygma*. But, whereas the Apologists (as also Clement and the Latitudinarians) were content to leave the common Christianity of their time intact, so far as it consisted in creed and ritual, the Deists on the other hand set their rational doctrine in opposition to everything that went beyond it. They claimed that it was not only the essence of Christianity, but also the only true Christianity. This contention was forcibly expressed in the title of two famous books, Toland's *Christianity not Mysterious* (1696) and Tindal's *Christianity as old as the Creation, or the Gospel a Republication of the Religion of Reason* (1702).

The particular strength of Deism was that, though in its inception by Lord Herbert it was affiliated to Stoicism, it showed a power of adaptability to the new philosophy which had arisen in the seventeenth century as a result of the great contemporary developments in natural science. In England the chief representative of a modern philosophy in the second half of the century was Locke, and with Locke's philosophy Deism entered into a firm alliance from the time of Toland onwards.

The Deists, however, had trouble over their complete identification of Christianity with the religion of reason. There stood in the way, not only the Creeds, but still more the New Testament. Here was the critical issue for Deism.

At this point great importance attaches to Locke's book, *The Reasonableness of Christianity as delivered in the Scriptures* (1695). Here Locke strives to mediate between Deism and the older theologies, in which task he is influenced by both Arminianism and Socinianism. He says that the New Testament shows clearly that the one necessary article of faith is that Jesus is the Messiah, including as its concomitants belief in His resurrection, rule and coming to judgment. In other words, even more definitely than Socinus Locke proposes to return to the *kerygma*. But he has a different way of dealing with Paul's Epistles. Instead of the forced exegesis of Socinianism he puts the 'occasional' character of the Epistles, making a critical distinction between them and the Gospels and Acts: a great deal in them is simply by way of accommodation to the special needs of their readers and has no permanent value. There is here in an elementary form the principle of a critical New Testament theology such as we have to-day. All that has been done since Locke's time is to work out the consequences of the principle more thoroughly than he was able to do, and with a scholarship greatly increased beyond that of the seventeenth century.

The Deists were not slow to take advantage of the new method introduced by Locke; they proceeded by its help still further to rationalize the doctrine of the New Testament. This is done, for example, in Chubb's *Posthumous Works* (1748). Here Christ's Messiahship is reduced to a Divine mission to instruct men in the moral law and to teach that there are rewards and punishments after death. He was a man like all others. The resurrection story is full of difficulties. What is meant by the Holy Spirit is by no means clear. Here even the *kerygma* has disappeared. Deism stands out in its naked simplicity as all that is left of the New Testament when Chubb has finished with it. And therewith the whole structure of dogma reared upon it falls to the ground. The Trinity is an impossible idea. Chubb calls it the doctrine of a 'triangular' God, referring to a representation of the Trinity painted on or over the altar-pieces in some churches (*op. cit.*, II, p. 178).

Here the Antitrinitarian movement reaches completion. It only remains to be observed that the rationalism of England spread to Germany, and there in the eighteenth century became the Aufklärung or Illumination, now adapting itself, instead of to the philosophy of Locke, to that of Leibniz as popularized by Wolff. The change made no theological difference, since both Locke and Wolff found room for theism in their several philosophies. But the Aufklärung made an advance upon Deism in that it proceeded to apply the method of historical criticism, not merely to the New Testament, but also to the subsequent dogma. It was the time when Semler (1723-1791) really set historical criticism in full motion, devoting to it his whole energies and establishing it as an independent branch of theological science. The Aufklärung also saw the birth of the 'quest for the historical Jesus'. It was the assumption of Deism and of the Aufklärung alike that Jesus had Himself taught just exactly as they did. It was a natural consequence of such a view that the effort should be made to discover by a critical analysis of the Gospels, whether indeed He was what they said or not. And so with the publication of the Wolfen-büttel Fragments (1778) there began the great series of 'Lives of Jesus', written from the human point of view, which reached its climax in the nineteenth century.

Rational theology in the seventeenth and eighteenth centuries culminated in Deism and the Aufklärung. But the instance of the Latitudinarians shows that the influence of the spirit of reason in the age was not confined to those who approached traditional Christianity only as iconoclasts. And as a matter of fact, it operated strongly among those who maintained the orthodox doctrine of the Trinity, in producing fresh endeavours to defend it on a rational basis. The outstanding instance of such operation was the Trinitarian controversy of the last two decades of the seventeenth century in England, when an incredible number of books, tracts and letters on the subject were published. A long list of the principal treatises is given by Hunt, *Religious Thought in England,* vol. II, pp. 273ff. In the preceding chapter Hunt gives an account of the controversy. The centre of it was a dispute between Sherlock and South (*op. cit.,* pp. 203-212).

Sherlock's treatise was *A vindication of the Holy and Blessed Trinity and the Incarnation of the Son of God* (1690). In it the author made use of the notion of self-consciousness, recently made the starting point of philosophy by Descartes. It is self-consciousness which constitutes the numerical oneness of a finite spirit. Such a spirit is not conscious of the thoughts of another similar spirit. But the case is different with Infinite Mind. Here, as Scripture makes plain, we have three Infinite Minds or Self-consciousnesses, really distinct from one another, and yet entirely each one conscious of the thoughts of the others, so that they may be said to be numerically one. Thus may be explained the mystery of the Trinity as set out in the Athanasian Creed. There is perfect harmony between the three Persons: but their unity is more than moral, it is a unity of specific nature. There is no difficulty at all, if God is thought of as a simple act or energy. It is evident that Sherlock's doctrine is that of the

Cappadocians interpreted through the principle of self-consciousness and so modernized.

South, disagreeing with this modernization of the doctrine wrote *Arimadversions upon Dr. Sherlock's book entitled a Vindication of the Ever Blessed Trinity* (1693). He proposed to clear the doctrine from Sherlock's 'new notions and false explications'. He defended the doctrine of three Persons or subsistences with one Essence. It is not enough to say that God is Infinite Mind. If this be all, He is not a substance, and if He is not a substance, is nothing. Nor are Person and self-consciousness equivalents. Self-consciousness presupposes personality, which is different from it. The difference may be seen by contemplating the human nature of Christ which is perfectly conscious of all its internal acts and yet taken by itself is not a person. Besides, Sherlock's theory would as well prove three thousand persons in God as three. Sherlock answered that the number three came from Scripture, and his object was to show how the three might be one.

It is impossible here to recount all the different positions taken by those who engaged in the controversy. But that of Wallis, the Cambridge mathematician, should not be overlooked, since it is the absolute opposite of that of Sherlock. Wallis wrote a series of *Letters on the Trinity* (Hunt, *op. cit.*, pp. 205f.). In the first of these, published in 1690, he said that the doctrine of the Trinity was rationally explicable. It must be recognized that 'Person' in the doctrine of the Trinity has not the same sense as when it is applied to a man. It simply stands for a distinction such that one Person is not another Person, and yet all are only One God. How this may be possible may be illustrated from a cube, which has three dimensions and yet is only one cube. So also to be, to know and to do are all distinct from one another, and yet it is the same soul that is, that knows and that acts.

Sherlock's doctrine was condemned by the Heads of

Colleges in Oxford as heresy, but he was unmoved by the condemnation. The time was one of great exercise of reason in theology in all directions. One form that it took was a re-examination of the patristic doctrine of the Trinity. The Continental Arminians, Episcopius and Curcellæus, had maintained that the Ante-Nicene Fathers had a doctrine different from that of Nicæa. Their aim was greater freedom of doctrine. But the Jesuit Petavius supported the same thesis with a view to proving the right of the Church to make fresh decisions in matters of doctrine. In 1685 appeared Bull's famous *Defence of the Nicene Faith*, which argued that there was no doctrinal difference between the Ante-Nicene Fathers and the Council of Nicæa. But in spite of his arguments, the matter was reviewed by Whiston and Clarke in the early eighteenth century. The latter published his treatise *The Scripture Doctrine of the Trinity* in 1712. As a result of this book an Arian controversy followed in England upon the Trinitarian controversy just described, and throughout the century Arianism made considerable inroads upon orthodoxy. This second controversy is described by Hunt (*op. cit.*, Vol. III, pp. 13ff.).

4. THE REGENERATION OF THEOLOGY

On the Continent the seventeenth century was the time of the great scholastic systems of Protestantism. But in Germany already by the side of them there was developed the Pietistic movement, led by Spener (1635-1705) and Francke (1663-1727), which without denying the truth of orthodox Lutheran doctrine insisted that what most mattered was spiritual experience, a matter of the heart rather than of the mind. One may compare the Quaker insistence in England about the same time on 'truth' as a matter of life in the Spirit, and not of 'notions', or dogmatic formulæ. Pietism and Quakerism are both of them to be reckoned to the antidogmatic movement. Quakerism was expressly antidogmatic, and Pietism at least made doctrine secondary to experience. One result of Pietism was the Moravian Church, where in combination with the organizing power of Zinzendorf, it found a fitting and adequate vehicle for the display of its energies. It was the Moravian form of piety, that seizing upon the spirit of John Wesley created the Evangelical Revival in England, and which impressing the young Schleiermacher became a potent factor in the regeneration of theology in Germany. To the study of this regeneration of theology we must now turn.

Here at last we come to the modern theology of our subject. What exactly do we mean when we speak of modern theology? In a sense all new theology is modern as compared with that which went before it. Thus in the later Middle Ages the Thomists and Scotists were called the *antiqui,* the Occamists being the *moderni.* But for all that the phrase 'modern theology' to-day has a special meaning which goes beyond this general distinction of new and old. To see what this meaning is, we must review the course of theology up to the eighteenth century from the point of view of the changing relations in it of the factors of authority, reason and experience, which have been recognized as constantly determining its character. It is by the proportions in which they enter into any particular theology that they determine its character throughout. What is meant may be illustrated from the child's toy called the kaleidoscope, in which a particular collocation of pieces of coloured glass was reflected in a triangle of mirrors, so as to multiply the pattern on every side. Just so is the special relation of authority, reason and experience in a theological system reflected in all its parts.

Let us then recall the way in which these factors have been related in the theologies we have so far studied, noting the changing positions assumed by them, and coming gradually to the relation into which they were at the end of the eighteenth century. It is this peculiar relation that constitutes 'modern theology' in its contrast to everything that went before.

We saw that in the charismatic theology of the New Testament authority and reason are both in evidence, while the creative power came from the experience of the Spirit (Gal. i. 10; I Cor. ii. 10, xii. 3; Jn. xvi. 13; I Jn. ii. 20; Rev. i. 10, 11). We saw further that in the great development of dogma which followed upon the charismatic age, authority and reason came to the front, while experience retired into the background. It was compared to a Cinderella; and we may say that it tended the hearth, and kept the home fires burning. We have seen how in the end it was by their saving power that different and competing forms of doctrine were tried. At the Reformation the principle of experience, which had previously found expression in medieval mysticism, was associated by Luther with his gospel of justification by faith. But we saw that Calvin reduced 'the testimony of the Holy Spirit', which Luther had invoked, simply to a support of Scriptural authority. Other Protestant theologians did the same, and so, just as in the dogma of the Ancient Church and the medieval scholasticism based upon it, authority and reason once more came into full power, the result being the Protestant scholasticism of the Continent, Lutheran and Calvinist. Thus in the sixteenth and seventeenth centuries four great orthodoxies, Greek, Roman, Lutheran and Calvinist, stood face to face; while the Church of England mediated between Catholicism and Protestantism, with the consequence that those Dissenters who desired a more Protestant type of religion were compelled to leave it.

We have seen further how reason, which had greatly developed its powers of criticism in the Middle Ages under the shadow of authority, was liberated from the pressure of that authority by the Renaissance. The first result was the grammatico-historical exegesis of Erasmus, and the further consequences were Socinianism, Arminianism, Latitudinarianism, Deism and the Aufklärung. Meanwhile also the principle of experience reasserted itself in Quakerism, Pietism, Moravianism, Methodism and the Evangelical Revival. But so far there was no theology adequate to the new situation. The Latitudinarians had fallen back on Neoplatonism, so as to find room for experience. The Deists had returned to the theology of the second century Apologists. Pietists, Methodists and Evangelicals remained generally true to the theology of Protestantism, if not Lutheran or Calvinist, at least only modified as far as Arminianism. Barclay, the Quaker, certainly wrote a notable system of theology, *An Apology for the true Christian Divinity*, in which he gave the inward illumination of the Spirit priority over both Scripture authority and natural reason, though he said that there could be no contradiction of them in such experience. But the *Apology*, written in 1676, whatever its merits or defects, could not be adequate to the situation as modified by the historical criticism of the New Testament, which Barclay could not anticipate.

The beginnings of this criticism have been spoken of already. To what has been said of Locke, Chubb and Semler, it may be added that even earlier in 1670 the philosopher Spinoza had enunciated the principle of historical criticism as regards the Old Testament in his *Tractatus theologico-politicus*, where he insisted that in the interpretation of the prophets the circumstances of the time and its ruling ideas must be taken into account. The historical criticism of the Scriptures is a factor which has immensely changed the problem of Christian theology since the days when the dogma was formulated. The modern position has been recognized in the treatment of the theology of the New Testament as charismatic, and as utilizing the current ideas of its time. Of course since Spinoza, Locke and Semler the historical criticism of the Scriptures has been developed enormously. Beginning as a small seed, it has grown, not merely into a tree, but into a whole forest of arguments and positions, the end of which is not yet. This development must be presupposed as accompanying that of the modern doctrine presently to be described: notice will only be taken of fresh critical results where they come into the picture.

The new stress on experience and the advance of historical criticism, taken by themselves, are not sufficient to make modern theology: they only create its problem. To complete the making of modern theology there had to be added the transforming effect of reason upon the framework in which up to the end of the eighteenth century theology in general had been set. This framework was the rational theology of the early Christian Apologists with its doctrines of God, the moral law and immortality. Except for doubts voiced by Ockham at the end of the Middle Ages, it had stood as the invariable foundation of theology. We have seen that it was all that the Deists and the Aufklärung in their iconoclastic zeal left standing.

The end of the Aufklärung came with the philosophy of Kant. It is the impact of this philosophy upon the rational preamble to theology that has brought about the modern theological situation. Even where the Kantian philosophy has been disowned, its influence has been felt. Natural or rational theology has never been the same since his time. It came down to Kant as it had been finally set out in scholastic form by Wolff, the great philosophical authority of the Aufklärung, and it stood as a rational theology, cosmology and psychology, together with a rational ethic. All these doctrines Kant criticized and transformed. The result of his work was

L

ultimately to compel a reconstruction of the whole theological fabric. We have therefore at this point to deal with the Kantian philosophy, just as earlier on we had to study the thought of Hellenism.

It is no wonder that Kant's philosophy should transform the entire theological situation at a time when reason and experience were both of them pressing their claim against authority. For the very philosophical problem to which he devoted his extraordinary mental energy was just that of the relation of reason and experience in general.

Let us consider how the problem came to him. We must go back to Descartes with his principle of self-consciousness. In an age of uncertainties he found 'I think, therefore I am' to be a certainty from which he could advance to others and build up a rational system of philosophy. He was interested in epistemology only as a means to an end, which was metaphysic. On the Continent Spinoza, Leibniz and Wolff all followed the same line of rationalism. But in England it was different. So far Locke has been spoken of only as a prop of the natural theology of Deism. But his great interest was in epistemology based on a critical analysis of experience. He was followed in this work, first by Berkeley, and then by Hume: in the hands of the latter it led to a scepticism that left nothing standing but mathematics and matters of fact. Books on metaphysic and school divinity were only worthy of the flames.

Between Wolff the rationalist and Hume the sceptic lay Kant's problem. He solved it by a critical philosophy that found room for both rationalism and empiricism. This philosophy he gave to the world in a series of astonishing works, all written in the decade 1781-1790. The first and most fundamental of all was his *Critique of Pure Reason*. Here his point of view is taken up at the very beginning, when he says 'Though all our knowledge begins with experience, it does not follow that it all arises out of experience'. The analysis of experience in fact discloses in it, not only a raw material of sensible impressions, but also certain rational forms by which it is organized and converted into knowledge. The first of these forms are the intuitions of space and time: external experience is both spatial and temporal, internal experience is temporal only. But besides these intuitive forms of experience, Kant also found it further organized in a rational way when we state our knowledge in the forms of judgment using certain fundamental organizing notions which have been tabulated in Logic. These notions he called the categories of the understanding, since it is by means of them that we understand. Foremost and most important among them are the notions of substance and cause. The answer to the scepticism of Locke about substance and of Hume about cause is that these notions have their rightful place in the organization of experience into knowledge. Knowledge undoubtedly exists in the form of mathematical physics, and it is not possible except by means of these categories.

Wolff's metaphysical system, however, stood for great Ideas altogether transcending any possible experience, which were the product of reason only. Kant accordingly distinguished between the categories of the Understanding through which experience is understood as it is given to us, and the Ideas of Reason which seek to go beyond it in order to complete it. Following Wolff's order of thought, he defined the Idea of the World as the totality of external experience, the Idea of the Soul as that of internal experience, and the Idea of God as the totality of both external and internal experience. Kant's general criticism of all the Ideas was that because they transcend any possible experience, they can never constitute or organize experience as do the categories in our understanding of it: all that they can do is to direct the advance of knowledge, they are regulative of our thought.

In the *Critique of Practical Reason*, the second of the three Critiques, Kant found a roundabout way of recovering what had been lost in the *Critique of Pure Reason*. He discovered in reason a moral law directing human conduct, which transcended all experience and was yet incontrovertible. Its word was 'Thou shalt'. Duty was absolute, and there was no 'If' about it, no limiting condition whatsoever. But how could man, thus subject to the demands of the law, and yet possessed by an instinctive and unquenchable desire for happiness, live as a moral being in a natural order which appeared to be governed, not by the moral law, but by the physical law of causation?

Kant found the solution of this problem in the moral law itself. It is absolute; and so what it requires must be. But if we are to obey it in a world governed by the laws of nature, we must postulate not only our own freedom of will, but also an Almighty Power over nature, acting in harmony with the moral law. In other words we must believe in a Righteous God as the Creator and Ruler of the World. Moreover, since the infinite task of duty transcends the possibilities of mortal life, we must also postulate the immortality of the soul.

Further, the moral law, being absolute and independent of particular conditions, is universally the same in all men, who therefore in their regard for the law must also respect other men as its bearers. Thus we come to the notion of a society of moral beings, directed and supported in their obedience to the moral law by God: we have, in other words, the sum of moral action as a Kingdom of God.

The two Critiques of Pure and Practical Reason may be regarded as the two halves of a new Logos doctrine. In ancient philosophy Logos (or Reason) was immanent both in the world and in the mind of man. In Kant's system Reason (or Logos) is immanent as Pure Reason in the principles of our knowledge of the world, man included; while as Practical Reason it is immanent in man's mind in the moral law, which is under God the organizing principle of His Kingdom in the world. The similarity with the old Logos doctrine is plain, but so also is the difference. What in ancient philosophy was one, is now in two parts. Reason appears to be divided against itself; and we know on the best authority that a house divided against itself cannot stand.

In the third Critique, the *Critique of Judgment*, Kant did something towards restoring the unity of reason. He found in the absoluteness of Beauty a symbol of the control of the sphere of sense by the moral law, and he also found a teleology in nature which foreshadowed the moral teleology of the Kingdom of God.

On the other hand in his book *Religion within the bounds of Pure Reason*, Kant found a new and worse breach between reason and sense than anything previously mentioned. Here reason takes the breach into itself by making inclination and not duty the maxim of conduct. Instead of the ideal of the Kingdom of God we have a radical evil in the will as the reality in human existence. This is what Christianity calls sin, but at the same time has a gospel of redemption. So in his own way has Kant. His philosophical principle that what ought to be must be, allowed him to speak of salvation by faith in the moral ideal as realized, which he said might be described in a figure as 'the Son of God come down from heaven'. At the same time he recognized the value of Jesus as a moral example. On the other hand his cool and severe moral judgment mistrusted as fanatical all dependence upon the recreative power of the Holy Spirit, and he regarded the doctrine of the Trinity as of no practical value. By his Critiques Kant had made an end of the Aufklärung, and yet in religion he got little further than the Aufklärung. He was like Moses, who led the children of Israel through the wilderness, but never entered the promised land.

To go beyond Kant two things were necessary; the first was to unify his new Logos doctrine more thoroughly than he had been able to do, the second was to do a justice to religion and Christianity that he had not done. The first task was the concern of the post-Kantian German Idealism, of which Fichte, Schelling and Hegel are the outstanding representatives. But the second task was achieved, not by these philosophers, but only by the modern theology, which starting out of the midst of the Idealist philosophy, originated with Schleiermacher.

We begin with the Idealist efforts to unify Reason, and so as a consequence to unify the world. Fichte in his highly original *Grundlage der gesammten Wissenschaftslehre* (1794) analysed self-consciousness, and found that the self or Ego first distinguished within itself an opposed Non-Ego, and then proceeded to resume the Non-Ego into itself. By this principle of division and reunion, Kant's two Critiques of Pure and Practical Reason were to be made one, the former as the sphere of the diremption of the Ego, the latter as that of the restoration of its unity. Schelling, following upon Fichte, applied the new principle to the Universe, where the drama of Ego and Non-Ego was worked out on a cosmic scale in the antithesis of Spirit and Nature and their ultimate Identity. Hegel took from his predecessors the general principle of Thesis, Antithesis and Synthesis as the very nerve of thought, and proceeded by means of it to explain all things in heaven and on earth in the most completely rounded philosophical system of modern times.

Here were then in the philosophies of Fichte, Schelling and Hegel three variant forms of the new Logos philosophy, now in them reduced to unity. But all three philosophers when they came to religion and Christianity, simply identified both essentially with the new Logos philosophy as they severally presented it. Fichte teaches that his *Wissenschaftslehre* raises Christianity from the sphere of historical fact to that of metaphysical truth. Schelling had a similar view with regard to his own philosophy. Hegel found a place for religion in his system as the presentation in the form of *Vorstellung* (i.e. Imagery) of what philosophy finally states in the perfect form of *Begriff* (i.e. Concept). From this standpoint Hegel set out to explain the anthropomorphisms of religion and to translate them into their philosophical meaning. It is obvious that the doctrine of the Trinity would lend itself with particular ease to interpretation in Hegelian terminology. There is a natural affinity between Hegel's philosophical triad and the Christian Trinity as psychologically illustrated by Augustine and Aquinas. Hegel equated the Father with the Absolute Idea as it is in itself before passing over into its opposite, the Universe which it generates out of itself, and which corresponds to the Son. The Spirit is the consciousness of the Idea which develops within the Universe; it is the Idea's self-knowledge reached as the result of the whole evolutionary process. We may note that Hegel speaks of the different stages in the unfolding of Thought as its 'Moments', points where it seems to pause before going on further.

5. SCHLEIERMACHER

It cannot be said that any one of the foregoing philosophers did adequate justice to religion and Christianity. To do such justice under the new conditions that have been explained is precisely the aim of all 'modern' theology. Thus we return from our long but necessary detour into philosophy to our subject proper and enquire what has become of the doctrines of the Trinity and the Incarnation under modern conditions, where authority has had to yield priority to experience as interpreted by reason, critical and constructive.

It has been explained that the transformation of

the framework in which Christianity was interpreted proceeded ultimately from the work of Kant. It was natural therefore that modern theology should begin in Germany, where also post-Kantian philosophy had its beginning. And indeed unquestionably ever since the early years of the nineteenth century down to the present time German theology has had the primacy over all other. Its hegemony in modern theology resembles that of Greek patristic theology in the Ancient Church, and is grounded on a similar reason. Just as Greek philosophy furnished the framework of the traditional dogma, so philosophy as transformed by Kant has furnished that of modern theology. The difference is that in the spheres where modern thought obtains, disagreements are no longer settled forcibly by Church Councils.

Our next work, therefore, is to study the modern German theology of our subject. Here three names stand out above all others, those of Schleiermacher, Ritschl and Barth. Apart from the special genius of these three theologians, which is great, their theology and indeed other German theology, has the merit of being fully systematic and thoroughly worked out with no loose ends. Of the three Schleiermacher, justly called 'the father of modern theology', is the greatest. The other two, even though they protest against him, Ritschl less, Barth more, do not escape his influence. Ritschl subscribes to his method of religious experience (*Justification and Reconciliation*, E.T., pp. 8f., 34). And though Barth repudiates any connection with the line Schleiermacher—Ritschl—Herrmann (the last his Ritschlian teacher), yet in his book *Die protestantische Theologie im neunzehnten Jahrhundert* (pp. 379, 380) he speaks of Schleiermacher as 'the great man', and admits that it is impossible to say whether even yet theology has got beyond his influence. He says that the nineteenth century was his century as a whole, and that it is doubtful if we are not still children of that century at bottom, in spite of all protestation against it and him. It is most necessary, therefore, for us to understand Schleiermacher, even though at first our study may appear to go wide of the doctrine of the Trinity. It will not do so in reality, even when we are discussing the first principles of his theology. The modern way of looking at both the Incarnation and the Trinity depends upon the general revolution in theology introduced by Schleiermacher, which was as great as the philosophical revolution initiated by Kant.

All the factors that contribute to modern theology met in 'the father of modern theology', though of course they did not make him; what did was his own genius. But he grew up in the age of the Aufklärung, with its historical criticism, the same in principle as ours, if less developed. He was educated at a Moravian school, where he learned the value of religious experience. Finally, he shared to the full in the philosophical movement of the time. He studied Kant, Fichte and Schelling and was a contemporary of Hegel. What we have to note, however, is that he also himself developed yet another variant of the Logos philosophy which aimed at the unification of the Kantian Critiques.

Our first concern, therefore, must be with this philosophy, which forms the link between the general philosophical movement and the theology which it helped to fashion. Schleiermacher's theological system, 'The Christian Faith', is best understood, not from his famous *Speeches on Religion*, especially in their original form, representing the philosophy of his youth, but rather from his metaphysical *Dialektik*, posthumously published in 1839. Schleiermacher stands out from the other philosophers of the movement in which he shared, because he gives an independent value to religion, and indeed finds in it the means of unifying the Kantian dualism of reason. His claim for the independence of religion goes

back to the *Speeches*, but it is in the *Dialektik* that we are
made to see its metaphysical import. Religion is seen as
the revelation of the transcendent unity beyond the
dualism. Schleiermacher's Moravian education had opened
up to him a further 'dimension' that had escaped the
notice of Kant.

The *Dialektik* distinguishes between two attitudes in
which we stand to the world. In knowledge we are determined by it, in action we determine it. The two attitudes
are starkly opposed: how is it that both are possible to
us? It is because in passing over from the one to the other,
we pass through a point which is neither knowledge nor
action, where recollected into the root of our being we are
for the moment one with the world in the root of its being.
This point is then a feeling of absolute dependence, which
is the same thing as the consciousness of God, and is the
essence of religion, which though itself unmetaphysical,
has metaphysical value in that it reveals God.

God is the ground of the Universe, which proceeds
from Him in the two hemispheres of nature and spirit.
Abstractly viewed, the former hemisphere is described in
the laws of nature; concretely viewed, it is all the variety
of nature itself. As to the second hemisphere, abstractly
regarded it furnishes the system of ethics; concretely
regarded it is the process of history.

The mention of history brings us to another special
difference of Schleiermacher's philosophy. He not only
put a metaphysical value upon religion, but also a special
revelational value upon history. He was not prepared like
Fichte and others to sublimate the historical element in
Christianity into metaphysical truth. Metaphysics provided the framework for his theology, history gave its
content. Schleiermacher was helped here by the thought
of Herder, the contemporary of Kant, who in his *Ideen zur
Philosophie der Geschichte* had insisted upon the importance of history as the sphere of Divine manifestation

and had protested against the reduction of religion to abstract ideas.

Schleiermacher's great classical work, the fountain head of all modern theology is *Der christliche Glaube* (*The Christian Faith*, 1821, 2nd ed., 1831; E. T. not till 1928!). It begins with propositions borrowed from Ethics, the Philosophy of Religion and Apologetics. It is these 'borrowings' that fit the theology into the philosophical framework. In his *Philosophische Sittenlehre* (*Philosophical Ethics*, posthumously published 1834-5) Schleiermacher explains that individuals symbolize their religious feeling in different ways, thus finding a means of communication with others. A church is a society of those who are drawn together in sympathy through such communication. The Christian Church is such a society based on a community of experience which is expressed in the symbols of a common faith. It is to describe the elements of this common faith that Schleiermacher goes on to the Philosophy of Religion and Apologetics. Religion is defined as the feeling of absolute dependence in the way that has been described already, but now Schleiermacher is further concerned with the manifestation of religion in history, the importance of which Herder had pointed out. Religion in history takes various forms, which stand on different levels. Schleiermacher divides the historical forms of religion, according to the clearness with which they express the God-consciousness, and according as they are non-ethical or ethical (or as he says aesthetic or teleological). The highest form of religion is that which is monotheistic and ethical. Christianity fulfils both conditions, since it is not only monotheistic, but also has a teleological structure, its religious-ethical end being the Kingdom of God. But even so we have not yet reached the peculiar essence of Christianity. It has to do with Jesus, and more than that with Jesus as Redeemer. We come to Schleiermacher's famous definition of the Christian religion (§ 11, *op. cit.*,

E.T., p. 52):'Christianity is a monotheistic faith belonging to the teleological type of religion, and is essentially distinguished from other such faiths by the fact that in it everything is related to the redemption accomplished by Jesus of Nazareth.'

Now at last Schleiermacher has all the materials for his system of theology. Schelling in his *System des transcendentalen Idealismus* (III) writes: 'Cartesius said as a physicist: give me Matter and Motion, and out of them I will build you the Universe.' One could in a similar way represent Schleiermacher as saying: 'Give me the God-consciousness and Jesus as Redeemer, and I will construct you the whole system of Christian theology.' For that is precisely what he does. It is as if he put himself back at the very beginning of Christian history to build a charismatic theology *de novo*. It will be charismatic, since it is founded on religious experience; it will be theology, because it will be scientific. Schleiermacher distinguishes three forms of religious communication, the poetic, the rhetorical and the scientific. What he means may be illustrated by thinking of the Psalms, and the Epistles of Paul, as compared with the *Summa Theologica* of Aquinas, Calvin's *Institutes*, or Schleiermacher's own system. In the first case we have an expression of religious feeling which is an end in itself. 'I sing as the bird sings' describes this mode of utterance. In the second case we have the intention of persuading others, and argument up to a particular point. What unity there is among the different forms of expression proceeds from the underlying experience: it is not the result of a direct aim. But in the third case, that of theology proper, such unification is the aim. Theology smooths out the differences or even contradictions of poetical or rhetorical expression, to bring all into harmony by tracing everything to the common experiential roots.

It is because of his going back far enough into these

experiential roots that Schleiermacher's theology attains a simplicity that the older theologies which work at the direct reconciliation of patristic or Scriptural authorities can never attain. His system is indeed simplicity itself. The whole difficulty consists in the approach to his position. That is why so much time has had to be spent over it. Everything depends upon moving from the presuppositions of the theology governed primarily by authority and reason, with experience only in the background, to those of the theology formed by the action of reason upon experience, where in the end authority becomes explicable.

Schleiermacher's system has two parts. The first part consists of the exposition in detail of what is involved in the God-consciousness, as it is everywhere implied in the Christian religion. The consciousness of absolute dependence upon God yields the doctrines of the creation and preservation of the world and man, and of the ideal relation of God, the world and man.

The second part of the system has to do with Jesus as Redeemer. Redemption is necessary because in actual experience the ideal relation of God, the world and man is not realized. Although the God-consciousness is the highest form of consciousness which ought to dominate man's whole life, in actual experience it develops later than our consciousness of the world through the senses, and so fails to control this sense-consciousness. This is the state of sin, and its result is the misery of a divided personality.

At this point, however, the situation is changed by the entrance of Jesus into history. He fulfils the ideal destiny of man, since in Him the God-consciousness is dominant over the sense-consciousness. 'The Redeemer', says Schleiermacher, 'is like all men in virtue of the identity of human nature, but is distinguished from them all by the constant potency of His God-consciousness, which was a veritable existence of God in Him' (§ 94, *op. cit.*, E.T., p. 385). Redemption follows when Jesus communicates the power of His God-consciousness to others, so that they no longer suffer from the misery of a divided personality, but on the contrary share His beatitude. The Christian Church is the Society originally formed by this communication, which continually transmits the redemptive power of Jesus by means of the communications made by its members. The Holy Spirit is the common Spirit of the Church. Those who belong to the Church, being regenerated by the Spirit which indwells its members, are transferred from the state of sin to a state of grace.

What is the bearing of all this on the doctrine of the Trinity? Since the originating cause of the doctrine of the Trinity is always the idea entertained of the Incarnation, we may expect that Schleiermacher's new Christology will work out in a different way of looking at the Trinity from that of tradition. And so it is. He says that the doctrine of the Trinity is not an immediate utterance concerning Christian experience, but is rather a combination of several such utterances so as to express their coherence in the whole of Christianity. He tells us that the real purpose of the doctrine of the Trinity is just to gather up into one what has been said already of the unique God-consciousness of Christ and of the Holy Spirit in the Church. In a word, Schleiermacher would have us be satisfied with the Trinity of Revelation, rather than try to penetrate behind it into the eternal Being of God. So strongly was Schleiermacher impressed with the transcendence of God, that he put in a word for what he called the 'Sabellian' doctrine of the Trinity. But it is necessary to take the term here, as it is said, 'with a grain of salt': it is used not only loosely, but actually incorrectly. A reference to the special essay which Schleiermacher wrote on Sabellianism in 1822 (*Sämmtliche Werke*, Abtheilung I, Bd. II, pp. 485ff.) shows that by putting together a number of late patristic references to Sabellius and interposing a great deal of guesswork, he created a 'Sabellius' of his own imagination. He denies (p. 547) that Sabellius could have taught that Father, Son and Holy Spirit represented successive phases in the Divine existence, which is precisely what he did teach. Schleiermacher makes him say on the contrary that God is transcendent Unity (μονάς), whom we only know (1) as manifest in the Universe apart from Christ and Christianity, (2) in Christ, and (3) in the Church. In other words, the 'Sabellius' of Schleiermacher is just Schleiermacher himself transported to the third century.

A good many questions arise out of our study of Schleiermacher's theology. In the first place it may be recognized that it comes triumphantly out of the two fundamental tests continually referred to in our work: it does recognize fully the humanity of Christ, and it is assuredly monotheistic. But there are other tests by which it must be tried. The full title of Schleiermacher's book is *The Christian Faith Systematically Expounded in Accordance with the Fundamental Principles of the Evangelical Church*. These principles are generally understood to be the doctrine of justification by faith and the sole authority of Scripture. The relation of Schleiermacher's system to the former will come up when we go on to Ritschl. We now consider its relation to the latter. As a charismatic product, it does not profess to be an aggregation of Scripture passages; but does it show an adequate insight into the spirit of Scripture and express its essence in a modern way? Is it Scriptural in that sense?

We see at once that if we take the Adam of the Bible to stand for sinful humanity as a whole, Schleiermacher's theology has an obvious affinity with Paul's doctrine of the First and Second Adam: it has an affinity also with the Johannine doctrine of Christ as the revelation of God and the life and light of men: moreover it combines the

Pauline and Johannine lines of thought in a way that is strikingly reminiscent of the theology of Athanasius. Both theologies begin with the enslavement of man by sense, both end with his redemption by Christ. Soteriology is the dominant note in both cases. But the difference is also impressive. The interest of Athanasius centres in the doctrine of physical redemption by the Resurrection, with the impartation of the Spirit as a second thought: Schleiermacher's doctrine is entirely ethico-religious, tracing redemption to Christ's communication of the God-consciousness through the 'total impression' of His Person. Schleiermacher dismisses not only the Virgin Birth, but also the Resurrection, the Ascension and the Second Coming of Christ all to the periphery of doctrine, handing them over to be studied by the historical criticism of the New Testament. He says roundly of the last three (and the statement would apply to the Virgin Birth also): 'If the redeeming efficacy of Christ depends upon the being of God in Him, and faith in Him is grounded on the impression that such a being of God indwells Him, then it is impossible to prove any immediate connection between these facts and that doctrine' (*op. cit.*, E.T., p. 418).

Yet Schleiermacher is not so far away from the primitive form of Christianity as this negative statement might suggest, if taken alone. For the Resurrection and Ascension of Christ had value in the original *kerygma* as signifying Christ's Lordship and His victory over all His enemies, which is further expressed by His sitting at God's right hand. Schleiermacher seizes upon this phrase as expressing metaphorically what he takes to be the essence of the whole matter, viz. the peculiar and incomparable dignity of Christ raised above all conflict and manifested in His spiritual presence and enduring influence.

6. RITSCHL

Ritschl, to whom we come next, works with the same Kantian framework as Schleiermacher uses, but he keeps closer to Kant. He repudiates a metaphysic which is indifferent ultimately to the distinction between nature and spirit: this excludes Schleiermacher's metaphysic of a unity of both in a common ground reached through the feeling of absolute dependence. Going back to Kant, but taking religion seriously as does Schleiermacher, Ritschl substitutes for Schleiermacher's metaphysic a religious view of the world in which the supremacy of spirit over nature is assured through the key-idea of the Kingdom of God. Schleiermacher, says Ritschl, had this key in his hands, when he defined Christianity as a teleological religion, and made its end the Kingdom of God. But in working out his theology he failed to use the key. The framework therefore has to be remodelled. Ritschl's way of stating its internal relations is by means of a philosophy of value judgments.

Theoretical judgments (those of pure reason) are disinterested, though they are accompanied by a concomitant judgment of their value. Ethical and religious judgments are however independent judgments of value, involving feelings of pleasure and pain, in the former case determined by our relation to the moral good, in the latter by the presence or absence of Divine help in overcoming the limitations put upon the personal spirit by nature and human society. Religion as such is not necessarily ethical. But Christianity is, as Schleiermacher said, both monotheistic and ethical, uniting religion and ethics in the idea of the Kingdom of God, which is at once God's gift to men and their moral task. The religious-ethical dominance of spirit over nature which Christianity secures, Ritschl called 'lordship over the world', which he equated with eternal life, as the victory of spirit over the things of

M

time and sense. His thought is akin to that of I Jn. ii. 17.

It is the conception of the Kingdom of God which locks everything into place in Ritschl's framework for Christianity. It involves a definitely personal view of God in opposition to the vaguer conception of Schleiermacher, who himself recognized that his theism approximates to pantheism taken at its highest level. Ritschl, however, subordinating nature to spirit and cosmology to teleology, conceives God Himself as having His Kingdom as his own self-end. It is the purpose that He cherishes in eternity and for which the world is designed.

Jesus Christ is now set in the framework of the Kingdom in this all-embracing sense, by the recognition of Him as the Founder of the Kingdom in the world. He arises out of Israel, which already had the Kingdom of God as its end, but conceived it nationalistically and materialistically. Jesus lifts the idea of the Kingdom into spirituality and universality. It is futile to ask how He came to this position: we have to deal with Him as He stands before us in maturity. On the one hand He incarnates the perfect spiritual religion, knowing God as Father, while He is known to God as Son. On the other hand He makes the Kingdom His ethical vocation. In both ways He reveals the love of God, in His filial relation to God, and in His own love to men in which God's love to them is manifested. Therefore He is God's revelation in a human person, the Word of God made flesh; and as such He has the value of God. Like Schleiermacher Ritschl lays stress on the immanence of God in Christ, which He sees further manifested in His patience, which exhibits His Lordship over the world, translating Divine omnipotence into human character. He is in fact Lord as God is Lord, both of nature and of men in the Kingdom, so that from the first there was applied to Him the title of Κύριος, which in the Old Testament stands for God.

The conception of the Kingdom of God, with which we

have been concerned so far, gives us only one half of
Ritschl's view of Christianity. His *magnum opus* was in
fact a very large-scale work, *The Christian Doctrine of
Justification and Reconciliation* (1870, 3rd definitive
edition, 1889, E.T. of Vol. III, 1902). The foregoing study
of his thought is based on Vol. III, Chapters IV and VI,
together with the Introduction. But the greater part of
the book, as the title suggests, is taken up with justification
and reconciliation, i.e. with the forgiveness of sins (cp.
Rom. iv. 4–6). Ritschl says in a famous sentence that
'Christianity so to speak, resembles, not a circle described
from a single centre, but an ellipse which is governed by
two *foci*' (*op. cit.*, E.T., p. 11). Accordingly he treats of the
forgiveness of sins at great length, but in the end after
long discussion of different views, comes to the simple
result that the forgiveness of sins proceeds from a further
extension of the same love of God that founds the Kingdom, and is revealed in the love of Christ, who was
faithful to his ethical vocation, in spite of all opposition
of sinners, even to the endurance of the death on the Cross.
Ritschl quotes Bernard of Clairvaux, *Sermons on the
Canticles*, XX, 2: 'In His words he bore with contradictors,
in His deeds with spies, in His torments with mockers and
in His death with revilers. Behold how he loved.'

Ritschl treated the forgiveness of sins as a personal
matter between God and the sinner, whose sense of guilt
is removed by the revelation of God's forgiving love.
He recognized that Schleiermacher's doctrine of Christ's
communication of His God-consciousness was a renewal
of Abelard's doctrine of the Atonement, just as was his
own. But he found Schleiermacher's statement an insufficient account of God's personal action in Christ
(*op. cit.*, Vol. I, E.T., p. 468). He did not do full justice
to the Evangelical doctrine of justification or forgiveness.
Here Ritschl's criticism was just.

As regards the doctrine of the Holy Spirit, Ritschl

substantially agreed with Schleiermacher in relating the Spirit to the Christian community. He said that the Spirit was the ground of its knowledge of God and of its specific moral and religious life.

And now we are prepared to see how Ritschl understands the Trinity. As with Schleiermacher, the doctrine of the Trinity becomes a compendious statement of the whole of Christianity. It derives from the attempt to view it altogether, as it exists in the mind and purpose of God. The Kingdom is God's eternal self-end or purpose, and Christ as the Head of the Kingdom in the world is eternally one with that purpose. Ritschl interprets His pre-existence by saying that He exists for God eternally as that which He appears to us in time. 'But only for God, since for us as pre-existent, Christ is hidden.' (We may compare Col. iii. 3.) Ritschl says further that the same line of thought leads to an intelligible view of the Holy Spirit. The Spirit of God is the knowledge that God has of Himself in His own self-end. (We may compare here I Cor. ii. 10, 11.)

To round off the above doctrine of the Trinity (which comes from *op. cit.*, Vol. III, E.T., pp. 470–2), two things should be added. The first is that while Christ and the Kingdom are eternally present to the Divine knowledge and will, the individual members of the Kingdom are conceived as known to God in time, so that the uniqueness of Christ is fully recognized. The second point is that Ritschl says that God's standpoint in eternity is impossible for us to sustain; like Schleiermacher he would have us fix our minds on the Trinity of Revelation.

The theologies of Schleiermacher and Ritschl are the typical modern systems. They have the merit of securing our two desiderata, monotheism and the human person or subject in Jesus. Barth says that the nineteenth century was Schleiermacher's century, and this is true at least of German theology, even though in the latter part of the century he was overshadowed by Ritschl; after all Ritschl's theology is only a modification of Schleiermacher's. Moreover, the beginning of the present century, before Barth came on the scene, showed a return of German theology from Ritschl to Schleiermacher: we shall see the reason presently.

Meanwhile we have to note that although the older theology of the creeds maintained itself in Germany side by side with the modern type, it did not do so without being in part influenced by the newer views. One remarkable evidence of this influence is to be seen in the kenotic theory of the Incarnation, of which Thomasius was the outstanding exponent in his book *Christi Person und Werk*[2] (1852–61). Basing himself on the older Lutheran kenoticism and developing it further, Thomasius taught that the Divine Son of God in becoming incarnate put into abeyance for the most part the Divine attributes related to the world, i.e. omnipotence, omniscience and omnipresence, while He retained the immanent and essential attributes of Divinity, i.e. absolute power or freedom, holiness, truth and love—Thomasius thought in this way to secure the full humanity of Christ without leaving the ground of the orthodox doctrine of the Incarnation.

It was not only, however, from the side of dogmatic theology that the new emphasis on the humanity of Jesus made itself felt. The period between Schleiermacher and Ritschl saw the advance of what is perhaps the most important doctrine of Biblical criticism, viz. that the Synoptic Gospels have priority over the Fourth Gospel as sources for the history of Jesus and His teaching. One effect of this critical preference is to be seen in the various endeavours of the time to write the 'Life of Jesus' as a human personality in history, and also to present His teaching on a Synoptic basis. Ritschl had the advantage over Schleiermacher of coinciding with this development in New Testament criticism and in the study of the life and teaching of Jesus. If one factor in the difference of Ritschl from Schleiermacher was the general philosophical return to Kant in Germany from the post-Kantian Idealism of Hegel during the second half of the nineteenth century, another was the new emphasis on the Jesus of the Synoptics; the two factors appeared to meet in the idea of the Kingdom of God, preached by Jesus and philosophically grounded by Kant. A complete harmony between the teaching of Jesus and the Kantian philosophy seemed to be established in the Ritschlian conception of the Kingdom of God as a society of men in the present world, by Divine help serving each other in love. Christianity was explained as a religious-ethical movement within humanity founded by Jesus. Barth says that this modern theology, or as he calls it 'modernism', might have succeeded but for one thing—that was the presence of the Bible in the Church. It was as a matter of fact from the study of the Bible that the first effective attacks were made on Ritschlianism, which came under fire both from the right and the left, curiously enough in the same year, 1892.

On the one hand, Kähler in his book, *Der sogenannte historische Jesus und der geschichtliche biblische Christus*, contrasted the nineteenth century 'Jesus of history' with the whole Christ of the Bible, historical in the true sense of the word. On the other hand Johannes Weiss, Ritschl's son-in-law, in *Jesu Predigt vom Reiche Gottes*, challenged the religious-ethical interpretation of the Kingdom as preached by Jesus: he maintained that Jesus conceived the Kingdom in terms of Jewish Apocalypse. It was for Jesus no work of man, but a pure gift of God, shortly to appear by a transcendent act of Divine power: the ethics of Jesus were simply for His adherents in the short interim period until the coming of the Kingdom.

The ideas of Weiss were strongly sponsored in the

epoch-making book of Schweitzer, *Von Reimarus zu Wrede* (1906; E.T., *The Quest of the Historical Jesus*, 1910). The swing of the theological pendulum which resulted was extreme. Apocalypticism in the New Testament could no more be ignored or explained away as a temporary figure for the religious-ethical social gospel. A new era of New Testament theology, characteristic of the present century began. Eschatology came into its own and dominated the scene once more, even though there was a recession from the extreme theory of Weiss and Schweitzer in the view of Otto and Dodd that Jesus, preaching the Kingdom of God, was already the eschatological event realized in history.

Since the thought of God associated with Apocalypticism is altogether transcendent, it is not surprising to find a fresh emphasis on the Divine transcendence manifesting itself in twentieth century dogmatics and philosophy of religion. The first appearance of this tendency was in the return, previously mentioned, from Ritschl to Schleiermacher in the first years of the century. Ritschl had certainly conceived God as 'supramundane' in His moral exaltation over nature, but Schleiermacher regarded religion as transcending both knowledge and action, and God as transcending similarly both nature and spirit.

7. BARTH

Such was the general theological situation, when the tempo of the change from immanence to transcendence and from belief in social progress to an eschatological outlook was immeasurably quickened by the shock of the war of 1914–1918. The end of the Ritschlian supremacy in theology was marked by two most notable books. First came Otto's *Das Heilige* (1916; E.T., *The Idea of the Holy*, 1923) with its conception of God as the 'numinous' the Absolutely Other, the *mysterium tremendum et fascinans*.

Then, secondly, and even greater in its effect, there appeared Barth's *Römerbrief* (1918; E.T., *The Epistle to the Romans*, 1933), which from its second edition (1921) onwards introduced the era in Protestant theology in which we still live. The key-note of the Divine transcendence is struck when Barth quotes in the Preface to this edition the words of Eccles. v. 2: 'God is in heaven, and thou upon earth.'

Many influences have contributed to the Barthian theology, beginning with the criticism of Ritschlianism which we have been studying. But above and beyond all we have to see in Barth a resurrection and development of the thought of the Danish philosopher Kierkegaard (d. 1855), who revolted from Hegelianism as an attempt of Reason to compass all things within its ambit. Barth acknowledges the influence of Kierkegaard in the abovementioned Preface. In his *Dogmatik* of 1927 and his *Kirchliche Dogmatik* of 1932 the use of Kierkegaard's philosophy as the framework for his theology is very evident, even though in his latest phase Barth claims to be independent of any particular philosophy.

Kierkegaard's philosophy, so far as it concerns us, is contained in his *Philosophical Fragments* (1844; E.T., 1936) and the sequel *Concluding Unscientific Postscript* (1846; E.T., 1941). A beginning is made from Socrates, who believed every individual as rational to have truth within himself: it only needed to be elicited. But how if there be error, and the error is the man's own fault, so that the individual is both guilty and in bondage? Here only God can help him. The Eternal Creator must come into time at a particular moment of revelation as both Judge and Saviour, and there must be conversion and a new birth.

Not in any system of reason, but in subjectivity is truth to be found. From the point of view of Reason God is Unknown, Transcendent, Absolutely Different. Yet

Reason has a passion to transcend itself. Only in God can this passion be satisfied, for it proceeds from Him. He must reveal Himself by a descent to man's level, taking the form of a servant. This He has done in Jesus Christ. In this form, however, God is still unknown as far as Reason goes. The Incarnation is the Absolute Paradox. The revelation can only be recognized by faith, which is a 'leap' beyond all evidence, whether the immediate evidence of the senses in the case of a contemporary, or the evidence of tradition in the case of a non-contemporary. The 'leap' is equally great in either case, so that the contemporary has no advantage over the non-contemporary. But if faith is not a matter of evidence, then it is an affair of will, it is decision. Yet the revelation can also produce, not faith, but offence. It may produce either.

The way that Barth applies Kierkegaard's ideas in his theology is as follows: First of all, he agrees with Schleiermacher and Ritschl that theology is to be developed from within the Church: faith is required as its presupposition. Next, the subject of theology is the Divine Revelation or Word of God, which has three forms. It is firstly the Word as preached to-day by the Church, secondly the Word as testified to by prophets and apostles in Holy Scripture, and thirdly the Word in the experience of the believer, where faith is created by it. It is this last form of the Word that alone is direct revelation. The faith that it creates is first trust in God, then knowledge, and finally confession, which naturally expresses itself in the language of the Church, viz. that of Scripture and the creeds, but which also inevitably makes use of philosophy, because it has to make itself intelligible to the world outside the Church.

Dogmatic theology, however, differs from both confession and preaching in that it is a critical discipline corresponding to the special position which Scripture occupies in the Church as the norm of faith. It applies the Scripture witness to test the truth of the Word as preached to-day. Dogmatics therefore proceeds as an exegesis of Scripture, which however is not merely grammatico-historical, but is theological, since it treats Scripture as a form of Divine revelation. From the former point of view Scripture is entirely open to historical criticism, but from the latter it is the Word of God. Its content both in Old and New Testaments is Jesus Christ. In Him God is revealed as Lord. When this revelation is expanded we have the doctrine of the Trinity, and when that is expanded we have the whole of the Christian Faith.

Such is Barth's general point of view. It is set out, as above, in his *Kirchliche Dogmatik*, I, 1⁵ (1947), §§ 3, 4, and in his *Dogmatik im Grundriss* (1947), §§ 2, 3, 4.

It is in the expansion of the Divine Revelation into Dogmatic Theology that Kierkegaard's philosophy is introduced. However much Barth may claim to be eclectic in philosophy, in reality he remains extraordinarily faithful to Kierkegaard. Kierkegaard's philosophy of revelation gives the frame in which Barth sets the Biblical Jesus Christ.

The sections of the *Kirchliche Dogmatik* which are here particularly important for us are I, 1, § 8, which deals with God in His Revelation, and § 9 which is concerned with God's Triunity. According to Barth the way that the doctrine of the Trinity develops out of God's revelation in Jesus Christ is very simple. The Trinitarian conception of God follows at once from the fact that God is known as He reveals Himself. Apart from Revelation God is hidden and unknown. Analysis of what is included in Revelation yields (1) the Revealer, (2) the act of Revelation, (3) the state of Revelation [*Offenbarer, Offenbarung, Offenbarsein*]. These distinctions correspond to Father, Son and Holy Spirit in Scripture (and in the Niceno-Constantinopolitan Creed, as is shown further on in §§ 10, 11, 12).

To see how this is so, Barth interprets the Divine

transcendence as God's Freedom. God reveals Himself in His Freedom as Sovereign Lord (*Herr*), and as Absolute Will. God is therefore revealed as Personal, the JAHWEH of the Old Testament and the *Kyrios* of the New Testament. He shows His Freedom in assuming a form of revelation without in the least parting with His mystery or abandoning His power to reveal Himself otherwise. Even in the historical Jesus God preserves His sovereignty. In Him God is still present *incognito*. Only as God's revelation to the individual creates faith is Jesus known as Lord.

The Father, Son and Holy Spirit of Scripture and the creed are thus to be interpreted as God's freedom in revelation, in the form of revelation, and in the historical contingency of revelation. Barth describes them in Hegelian terminology as the three 'moments' of revelation. God is revealed as Father in the Son in whom He takes form; and as He communicates Himself in revelation He is Spirit. There is only One God, but there are three distinct modes of His Being (τρόποι ὑπάρξεως, *Seinsweisen*). The 'Persons' of the Trinity are not 'personalities'. The ancient and medieval conception of person does not correspond to the modern idea of personality: it lacks the mark of consciousness. There are not three consciousnesses in God: that is the worst kind of Tritheism. There is only one consciousness and one God in three moments of His Being. Monotheism is absolute. God is One in all His operations in the world.

Although Barth thus speaks of Modes of the Divine Being (*Seinsweisen*), he says that his doctrine is not Modalism, by which he here means not historical Sabellianism, but the 'Sabellianism' of Schleiermacher. The 'moments', he says, are not just phases of manifestation which do not touch the Divine Essence: they are necessary distinctions in the Essence, and as such they are eternal as God is eternal. Modelling his language on that of Anselm, *De Fide Trinitatis*, IX, he speaks of a *repetitio eternitatis in eternitate*. He goes on to deny that his doctrine is in any way speculative. It is simply the result of an analysis of what is in Scripture. The doctrine of the Trinity is certainly not found in Scripture; but it is required for the interpretation of Scripture.

We note that in spite of his opposition to Schleiermacher and Ritschl Barth agrees with them on two important points: (1) the doctrine of the Trinity is a compendium of the whole of Christianity; (2) it takes the shape of an endeavour to look at the Divine revelation *sub specie eternitatis*. But the fundamental difference of Barth's doctrine from that of his predecessors appears in the way that he explains the Incarnation, where he follows in general the creed and the patristic theology. Schleiermacher and Ritschl began with the historical Jesus and found God immanent in Him, Barth begins with God in the form of revelation, God the Word. The Word assumed a human potentiality, and became Jesus of Nazareth, an individual man (*op. cit.*, I, 2^3 (1945), § 15). Individuality belongs to human nature; without it there could have been no Incarnation. But the individuality is that of the God-man. Barth says in agreement with the Ancient Church and subsequent orthodoxy that in Jesus Christ the Word is the subject and the humanity is the predicate. In other words, he subscribes to the doctrine of *enhypostasis*.

With this note on the Barthian doctrine of the Incarnation we come to the end of what is needed to explain his doctrine of the Trinity. But a final and very important question now presents itself: How far is Barth, who condemns Schleiermacher and Ritschl as Modernists, himself of the same breed? The answer may be given in two stages:

(1) The Kierkegaardian-Barthian philosophy of revelation is only a variant of that of Schleiermacher with still

greater emphasis on the transcendence of God. Schleier-macher taught that God transcended both nature and spirit, but was known in religious feeling. According to Barth God transcends religion also, which is man's search for God (equivalent to Kierkegaard's passion of the reason for God). God is so transcendent that he touches man only in one point, Jesus Christ, as Barth says, 'perpendicularly from heaven' (*op. cit.*, I, 1, p. 348). But it is to be observed that this doctrine of transcendence requires the Kantian philosophy of the autonomous ego, or some variant of it such as Hegelianism, to act as a foil to itself. Without the autonomous reason which it challenges, it would float free in the ether of the Absolute, making no contact with earth anywhere. In other words, transcendence could not become revelation. It may be added that Barth's doctrine of the Divine *incognito* in Christ has a family resemblance to Ritschl's theory of value-judgments.

(2) So far then Barth has much in common with the two great previous theologians. But his difference from them comes out over the way in which faith expresses itself. Schleiermacher needs only the Jesus of history and the God-consciousness in their relation to man and the world. Ritschl requires the Kingdom of God as preached by Jesus and translated into the language of philosophy by Kant, together with God's fatherly forgiveness of sins. But Barth finds it natural that faith should express itself, not only in the testimony of prophets and apostles, but also in the patristic creeds and the Reformed Theology. This is the most debatable point of his system. If we agree, as we must, that we have in Scripture the classical and normative expression of the Christian faith, there still seems no reason that faith to-day must express itself in the same language, let alone that it should further be bound by the traditional exegesis of Scripture. Historical criticism, which Barth accepts, must play upon Scriptural

modes of thought as well as upon Scripture records of
history. As a matter of fact Barth does so allow it to play
when he identifies Father, Son and Holy Spirit with the
'moments' of revelation, its Subject, its Form and its
Contingency. The Scripture names, he says, are only
analogical.

The general conclusion then is that Barth is more of a
'modernist' than he admits, even if he is not quite so much
of one as Van Til makes out in his polemical work, *The
New Modernism* (1946). Barth owes a good deal to Ritschl,
who also made Christianity entirely a matter of revelation;
and he owes still more to Schleiermacher with his emphasis
on the Divine transcendence. All has been put through the
mill of Kierkegaard's philosophy. But there can be no
doubt that Barth, even if not a 'modernist', is certainly
'modern'.

8. MODERN ENGLISH THEOLOGY

With Barth we come to the end of our study of the
German theology of the nineteenth and twentieth centuries.
But it still remains to say something of theology in our
own country, all the more so as in recent years there has
been a remarkable Trinitarian development strongly
opposed to any form of Modalism.

Reference has been made already to the Deism of the
eighteenth century and to the revival of Arianism in that
century. These were only extreme forms of the rationalism
that characterized the age. But in the nineteenth century
the theological position was changed by the operation of
two great forces, both of them operating to strengthen
the orthodox doctrine of the Trinity and the Incarnation
in its hold over the Church. The first was the great
Evangelical Revival initiated by the Wesleys; the second
was Anglo-Catholicism, following on the Romantic
movement in literature, and specially associated with
Newman. Accordingly the historical criticism which had

now greatly developed in Germany, only very slowly affected Britain. Its full force was felt by a man of letters like Matthew Arnold, but only in small measure by the main body of Christians. The attempt to naturalize criticism in *Essays and Reviews* (1860) was tentative only. It was not in England, but in Scotland, that the advanced criticism of the Old Testament became a power through the work of Robertson Smith, yet only to be stoutly opposed as heretical.

In *Lux Mundi* (1889), however, at last a coherent English theology was put out with allowance at least for Old Testament criticism. It was the time when the Hegelian philosophy had successfully invaded Britain; and the essayists used it, as it had been naturalized by T. H. Green, to make a framework for the patristic doctrine of the Incarnation; while at the same time the limitations of Christ's knowledge in his earthly existence were explained by the adoption of the doctrine of *kenosis* in Gore's essay, 'The Holy Spirit and Inspiration'.

The type of Trinitarianism congenial to the new movement may be illustrated from R. C. Moberly, the author of the *Lux Mundi* essay, *The Incarnation as the Basis of Dogma*. He developed his doctrine of the Trinity in *Atonement and Personality* (1901), Chapters IV and VIII. The Unity of God is fundamental. Much popular thought about God is tritheistic and provokes Unitarianism as reaction. Light comes from the notion of Divine Personality, which cannot be a mere unity, but implies both subject and object and their mutual relation, which is one of Love. The unity in God is not the unity of number, but is the unity of the Spirit. This is Augustine's doctrine, clarified by the Hegelian notion of personality as subject, object and the unity of both in Spirit. In a long note (B) to Chapter VIII Moberly recognizes that the name 'Son' can only be used analogically of the pre-existent Logos; and he sums up by saying that the Incarnation as continued through the Holy Spirit involves God *above* man, *with* and *as* man, and *within* man. It is a remarkable anticipation of the Barthian doctrine of God as the Transcendent Subject of Revelation, the Fact of Revelation, and the state of Revelation. A further resemblance to what we have found in Barth is that Moberly's Trinitarianism is accompanied by an enhypostatic doctrine of the Incarnation. If Christ's Humanity were not that of Deity, it could not stand in an inclusive relation, as it does, to that of other men. Christ is a Divine Person, expressing Himself in terms of humanity.

So far then the new movement in theology in England had brought forth a degree of approach to Modalism in the doctrine of the Trinity, even if it was balanced by an enhypostatic doctrine of the Incarnation. The Modalism naturally followed from the Hegelian philosophy of the authors of *Lux Mundi*, the enhypostatic doctrine remained as a survival of Catholic tradition, a rock unsubmerged by the tide.

In a most interesting essay in the *Congregational Quarterly* (1925) entitled 'The Present Position of the Doctrine of the Trinity', pp. 8ff., F. R. Tennant commented on the inconsistency of a Modalist Trinitarianism and an enhypostatic Christology. It is not surprising that others should have thought the same. We have now to chronicle the remarkable theological development already alluded to, which is not only a complete reaction from any kind of Modalism, but is actually a revival of the social doctrine of the Trinity, previously found unsatisfactory by Aquinas when propounded by Richard of St. Victor in the Middle Ages. The outstanding representation of this type of doctrine is in the quite recent Croall Lectures (1943), *The Doctrine of the Trinity*, by Professor L. Hodgson.

We therefore finish our study with an account of this challenging book. The philosophical background is no longer Hegelianism. That is regarded as outmoded.

Philosophy has become empirical. But the theological situation has been changed also in another way. During the dominance of Hegelianism in Britain enormous strides have been made in historical criticism, which has advanced from the Old Testament to the New Testament, where it has compelled the revision of much formerly accepted. As a result of such criticism, the notion of a revelation in propositions has had to be abandoned in favour of that of a revelation in Divine acts interpreted by experience. But this means that Christianity, being itself founded on experience, is in a position to save the general empirical philosophy of the time from becoming sceptical for want of fixed principles. Christian theology can supply a key-idea, which can lock experience together into a coherent whole.

Jesus of Nazareth was at first accepted by His followers as the Messiah prophesied in Old Testament Scripture, but when the gospel was carried to the Gentile world, He was preached as having brought deliverance from sin and adopted sonship to God. This led to the conclusion that He must Himself be God; and this conclusion continues to be confirmed by the continued experience of adopted sonship in the Church. The earthly life of Christ is there-fore the human life of One who was more than human. The Nicene ὁμοούσιον is the philosophical equivalent of what in Phil. ii. 5–11 is expressed in the dramatic language of pre-existence, a doctrine which can only have a meaning if it means more than it says. In the Creed an impossible bit of history is translated into a timeless truth.

What then was the character of Christ's earthly life? It was a life of self-giving to the Father, through the Spirit. The doctrine of the Trinity arises when we project this life into eternity, thinking away the accidents of earthly existence. The humanity of Jesus is sufficiently safeguarded, if it is said that the Divine Son of God submitted to the limitations of body and mind due to

N

existence in the physical world at a particular time and place, so that His experience was conditioned by them. In eternity those limitations do not exist, but there is still the eternal self-giving of the Son to the Father through the Spirit.

The problem of the doctrine of the Trinity is to reconcile this view of the Divine life in eternity with the fundamental doctrine of the Unity of God. The unity of thinking, feeling and willing in the human spirit furnishes a useful analogy. The unity of the self is not any one of the three factors, nor a fourth factor added to them, but is the activity that operates in all three together in spite of the distinction between them. Furthermore, the world supplies a whole scale of organic unities from the atom upwards to human life, and suggests the possibility of a unity still higher and more intense than any natural unity. Christian experience demands such a higher unity as its explanation. Christianity began with a Unitarian theology, but its religion was from the first Trinitarian as an experience of adoption to share in the relation of the Son to the Father through possession by the Spirit: Father, Son and Spirit are experienced here severally as Persons in the full sense of the word. The unity of God is matter of reason and revelation, not of experience, and only has reference to God's operation in the world. Christian experience breaks through the numerical or mathematical conception of unity and compels a revision of the idea of unity. It results in a social conception of the Trinity, in which the unity transcends our thought, though the scale of organic unities previously mentioned may help us towards imagining it. It is the Trinity that we know, the Unity that thought strains towards. It will be noticed that this is the exact opposite of the position of John of Damascus, who says most decidedly that the Unity is the first point in our knowledge of God, and that the knowledge of the hypostases is subordinate to it.

Professor Hodgson defends his position by a review of the history of doctrine. The true relation of the Persons, Father, Son and Spirit is drawn out in Scripture. The Logos idea served to introduce Christianity to the Hellenistic world, but became unnecessary after Nicæa. It was in itself misleading, being formed from an illicit union of Hebrew and Greek thought, the former supplying the notion of personality, the latter that of emanation. Of the creeds, only the Athanasian is completely satisfactory. Augustine, Aquinas and Calvin are examined as classical instances of Trinitarian doctrine, with the result that they are satisfactory so far as they adhere to Scripture. Where they attempt a rationalization that tends towards Modalism, it is only by way of analogy. So far as it is more, Augustine is unsuccessful, Aquinas only succeeds by means of abstractions, Calvin suffers least from attempted rationalization, because he keeps closest to Scripture and avoids philosophical problems. It will be seen that Professor Hodgson's view of the history is altogether different from that previously taken in this book.

The final question that arises about all this English theology is how far it is to be called 'Modern' in the sense that the theologies of Schleiermacher and Ritschl are Modern. The answer to the question is like that to the same question about Barth. A Post-Kantian point of view is implied.

The starting-point of Moberly's theology is from the general position of *Lux Mundi*, so well defined in Scott Holland's essay on 'Faith' in that volume. Faith is the simple surrender of the soul to God, the adhesion of its spiritual sonship to its Father. But Faith has a history, and that history is recorded in Scripture as a history of the Divine revelation to which it responds. The Creeds answer the questions which were provoked by this Divine revelation, as time went on. This is substantially the same position as Barth's, when he says that the language of Scripture and the creeds are Faith's native speech. Moreover, Scott Holland and Barth are at one in admitting the rights of historical criticism, and the necessity of utilizing modern philosophy to explain the Christian Faith to our own time.

Professor Hodgson occupies the same standpoint. It does not matter in comparing him with Moberly, that the latter like the rest of the writers in *Lux Mundi* uses Neo-Hegelianism as a philosophical framework, while Professor Hodgson prefers an empirical philosophy as more up-to-date. For when he says that revelation is not given in propositions but in Divine acts to be interpreted by experience, the analogy with Schleiermacher and therefore the ultimate dependence upon Kant is manifest. It is of course an important difference that Professor Hodgson sets the Trinity where Schleiermacher puts the identity of Nature and Spirit. But the general resemblance of framework remains. In both cases God, though differently conceived, is the Principle that binds the universe into one, and so prevents philosophy from dissolving into scepticism.

POSTSCRIPT

LET us sum up our results, and try to draw a conclusion from them. The roots of Christological and Trinitarian doctrine lie far back in the charismatic theology of the New Testament. We have distinguished in it three types of thought forming the varying expression of the common Christian faith. The first is that of the original *kerygma* of Jesus as Messiah, which was based on Jewish monotheism and the Divine commission of the man Jesus of Nazareth as God's Representative. The second and third forms of thought came into existence when Christianity became a missionary religion: they resulted from the endeavour to translate the *kerygma* into an equivalent terminology intelligible to the Hellenistic world. To show the relation of Jesus as Messiah (or Christ) to God it was not found sufficient simply to express His Messianic function as universal Lordship. There was the question of His essential nature, to explain which two ways were taken. Either His filial relation to God as Messiah was carried back into eternity, or else He was identified with the Eternal Wisdom or Word of God: the Greek word Logos comprehensively stood for both God's thought and His utterance of it. It has been noted that the identification of Jesus Christ with the Logos was first adopted to prevent the risk of His Sonship being conceived as simply angelic. There was indeed a conflation between the ideas of the Son and the Logos, but a distinction is made between them in the Johannine theology. It should be added that the Spirit bestowed on the Church was also regarded as Divine, but as to how thought fluctuated.

In the second century the authority of the New Testament was added to that of the Old Testament, alone recognized previously by the Christian Church. A tension then arose between the three different types of Christology just described. It was the middle form that determined popular thought, being enshrined in the baptismal formula and developed in the baptismal confession or embryo creed. Philosophical theology on the other hand eagerly seized on the identification of Christ with the Logos, but the first result was to set up a tension with the *kerygma* on the point of His manhood. This tension was overcome, but a new one then manifested itself between the credal and the Logos Christologies, a tension which dominated the whole later patristic theology. The influence of the *kerygma* still operated to require monotheism, that of the Creed tended to the distinction of Father, Son and Spirit. The Logos Christology wavered between the two points of view. So to meet all requirements there was developed the great Trinitarian doctrine of One Essence in three Hypostases, or One Substance in three Persons. But the tension continued within the doctrine in the shape of two opposing emphases, one from the Creed on the distinction of the Hypostases or Persons, the other from the *kerygma* on the Divine Unity. The earlier creeds were replaced by the creed of Nicæa, and that by the Niceno-Constantinopolitan creed, more and more definite Trinitarian doctrine being taken into the creed. In spite of all changes, the credal statement remained an expansion of the baptismal formula of Father, Son and Spirit; yet the accompanying Trinitarian theology interpreting the creed, in spite of deviations towards emphasizing triplicity, constantly tended more and more to the subordination of the three hypostases to the Divine unity. The terms Logos and Spirit themselves helped this tendency by suggesting psychological analogies.

The crucial point in the argument is where the Greek

theologians in dogmatic thought moved on from the conception of Son to that of Wisdom or Logos. To avoid any suspicion of bodily division in God, the generation of the Son was explained by that of the Logos, and in consequence Father, Son and Spirit tended to be conceived as modes of existence (τρόποι ὑπάρξεῶς) within the Divine Unity.

Augustine's book on the Trinity furnishes a Latin parallel to the Greek theology, in which the tendency we have been describing is still more definite. One of the results of Augustine's work was indeed the Athanasian Creed, which simply sets out the tension between the doctrine of the three Persons and that of the Divine Unity. But the other result, and the more important, was the Trinitarian doctrine of Aquinas. He selected one of the many psychological analogies suggested by Augustine to ease the tension in the doctrine of the Trinity, and he developed this analogy into a completely rounded doctrine of the internal processes of the Divine Life. God eternally forms the Image of Himself, and unites Himself with that Image in Love. The Thomist *Tractatus de Trinitate* is the climax of the whole patristic and medieval development. It is essentially the doctrine of a Living God, the God of the Old Testament, philosophically explained on the basis of the charismatic theology of the New Testament. The *kerygma*, the Creed, and this doctrine of the Trinity are related after the pattern of the Hegelian thesis, antithesis and synthesis.

Trinitarian doctrine moved faster than Christology in the patristic period. The reason was that already, before definite theological reflection began, Christology had established itself in the form of the Creed, in continuance of the middle form of New Testament doctrine. Popularly Christ continued to be thought of as the Son of God who had descended from heaven, and all the refinements of Trinitarian doctrine never overpowered this view so far as Christology was concerned. The result was seen in the Christological controversies which for long never reached anything but negative results. Jesus Christ was the Divine Person who also was human, but how was the problem. Solution after solution was rejected: in the end the view that prevailed was that of *enhypostasis*, the Divine Son of God assumed human nature, but Jesus was not a human person. Alcuin expressed the doctrine in an epigram: 'In the assumption of the flesh by God, the person perishes, not the nature.'

The final result of the Patristic, followed by the Medieval, theology, was therefore to leave a great hiatus between the doctrine of the Trinity and that of the Incarnation. In the doctrine of the Trinity the Divine Unity predominated, but in its application to Christology it was obscured by the distinction of the Persons. The Reformation left the position untouched, but the contemporary Renaissance ultimately produced a criticism of orthodoxy which expressed itself as Socinianism, Deism and Illuminism. The result was a determined return to the *kerygma*. God, said Socinus, was One Person. The essence of Christianity, said Locke, is that Jesus is the Messiah.

Was then the rest of the charismatic theology of the New Testament and the whole subsequent labour of theology to go for nothing? The answer to this question was found by bringing to light the experience which lay at the root of it all. Whereas before theology had been conducted as a debate between authority and reason, now experience came to view as the link between them. By this means there was made possible a modern theology, which has three marks. (1) It accepts the historical criticism of Scripture and dogma. (2) It makes reference to experience; even when the emphasis is on faith as the gift of God, it is still conceived as a form of human experience. (3) In beginning again, not directly from authority, but from the experience behind the authority, it naturally makes use of modern philosophy instead of the ancient philosophy embedded in the authority.

We have studied five representatives of such modern theology. Moberly and Barth are content to revise the older position with its hiatus between a doctrine of the Trinity where the Persons are subordinated to the Divine Unity, and a doctrine of the Incarnation where this subordination is virtually ignored. In taking this stand, it is probable that they are representative of much theology of the present time. The reason for the position is well explained by Barth, when he says that Christian faith naturally expresses itself in the language of Scripture and the Creeds. This is so far true as these represent the history out of which we come and which still lives in us. But it is not the whole truth: it does not allow sufficiently for the theological reflection which both Moberly and Barth employ in dealing with the Trinity. It cannot be said to reflection: 'Thus far and no farther.' If it is employed on the doctrine of the Trinity, it must be employed on that of the Incarnation also.

Our three other representatives of modern theology behave more logically than Moberly and Barth. They attempt to get rid of the hiatus that vexes theology, either by adapting Christology to a firmly monotheistic Trinitarianism, or by adapting Trinitarianism to the credal Christology.

How are we to decide this issue, so important for the theology of our time? The principle adopted as fundamental in this book has been that, since all subsequent theologies stand as an interpretation of the original *kerygma*, it is by their faithfulness to the *kerygma* that they must be judged. But this one principle gives us two points by which theologies are to be tried: are they faithful to monotheism and to the real humanity of Jesus?

o

However closely the *kerygma* associates Jesus with God, however much it points beyond itself to a Divine character in Jesus, it is not so as to throw doubt on the fact that He is a man. Theology may, and indeed must, go beyond the *kerygma* in interpreting it, but it must not contradict it.

Let us begin with Professor Hodgson, who stands on the Athanasian creed. It would of course be quite wrong to identify his doctrine with popular Christology. Does he not say of Phil. ii. 5-11, that it must be interpreted by the substitution of a timeless truth for an impossible bit of history? But he does stand on the distinction of the Persons to the extent of reviving in a modern form the social doctrine of the Trinity, taught by Richard of St. Victor and rejected by Aquinas. God, says Professor Hodgson, is known to us in Christian experience as three self-conscious Personalities, the Unity of which we can only dimly imagine. This doctrine is open to objection on all three grounds of authority, reason and experience.

(1) *Authority.* John of Damascus, summing up patristic thought, says that what we know first is the Divine Unity, not the hypostases. Augustine agrees.

(2) *Reason.* The doctrine leaves us with no intelligible conception of God. What it offers is too much like the unknown emergent of the future, that crowns the series of emergent unities in Alexander's *Space, Time and Deity.*

(3) *Experience.* It must be denied that Christian experience is an experience of three distinct Divine Personalities. It is an experience of the One God through Christ in the Spirit. Theology can analyse out of the experience the mediation of Christ and the power of the Spirit, but in the actual experience all is fused into communion with God.

The Christology which the social doctrine of the Trinity is intended to save, is as unsatisfactory as the doctrine itself. It certainly has much authority on its side, though not the all-important authority of the *kerygma*. But it cannot be proved from experience, and it certainly has reason against it. If it is said that Christ is experienced as a Divine personality, because His sonship is not adoptive as ours is, the conclusion does not follow. The distinction between the two types of sonship means simply that the filial relation of Jesus to God was original and sinless, while ours is that of sinners reconciled to God through Him. Thus experience fails to prove the traditional Christology, while its theological development into the doctrine of *enhypostasis* is so complicated as to be rationally unintelligible. Popular Christology indeed simplifies the matter by turning the Incarnation into a Theophany. To avoid this danger, Professor Hodgson speaks of the Divine Person submitting to the limitations of human experience. But a human experience consists of thought, feeling and will, and on Professor Hodgson's own showing, the unity of these is a self where there is no room for a fourth factor such as a Divine Subject. We conclude therefore from all that has been said, that a different way of uniting God and man in Jesus must be found.

We therefore pass over to the opposite form of doctrine, that of Schleiermacher and Ritschl, which keeping close to the *kerygma*, begins with the human person of Jesus. Ritschl expresses His Messianic representation of God by saying that God is immanent in Him, so that He has the value of God. But if we ask how these things may be, we are driven back upon the doctrine of Schleiermacher, that there was in Him an absolute potency of the God-consciousness which constituted a Being of God in Him. So we come to rest in the only Christology satisfactory to-day in the light of historical criticism, Christian experience and modern philosophy.

Schleiermacher's doctrine of the Trinity is not as satisfactory as his Christology. The reason is not far to seek. It is in his unsatisfactory doctrine of God. Because he thought of God as the Identity of Nature and Spirit, he explained the 'Persons' in the Trinity as phases of Divine manifestation which do not touch the Divine essence. To rectify the situation, firstly, we have to assert with Ritschl the truth that God is Spirit, the Creator both of Nature and of finite spirits; secondly, we have to affirm the principle stated by Barth in substantial agreement with John of Damascus and Calvin, that God is as He reveals Himself, or in other words, He is eternally what He is in time. The doctrine of the Trinity must therefore carry back what we learn through the Divine revelation into the eternal Being of God.

Ritschl goes some way in doing this. He speaks of Christ as eternal in the mind of God, while men in general are not so; and he regards the Holy Spirit as God's knowledge of His own purpose in Christ. But Barth takes us further, and does so more satisfactorily. He says that Jesus Christ is the objectivity of the Divine Revelation (*Kirchliche Dogmatik*, I, 2, §13) and the Holy Spirit its subjectivity (*ib.*, §16). This then is what we have to carry back into eternity. Barth of course implies his own Christology. But his principle can be applied to that of Schleiermacher, with the help of the doctrine that God is Spirit. We may say that the Absolute Potency of the God-consciousness, which is the Being of God in Jesus, constitutes the objectivity of the Divine Revelation, God *for us*. Thus Paul says in II Cor. iv. 6 that God shines in our hearts, to give the knowledge of Himself in the face of Jesus Christ. But then through Jesus God communicates Himself to us in the Holy Spirit, and this is the subjectivity of Divine revelation, God *in us*. So Paul says again that the love of God is shed abroad in our hearts through the gift of the Spirit (Rom. v. 5). Altogether then, God who is Spirit is revealed as Light and Love, and we have the sublime simplicity of the Johannine Trinity, Spirit, Light, Love. Or since all these modes of the

Divine Being are one and the same, we can say with
Charles Wesley: 'God is Love, I know, I feel.' The revelation is light to the mind and warmth in the heart.

When we carry back our profit from the Divine Revelation to God as He is in Himself, what at once suggests
itself is the classical doctrine of Aquinas that God eternally
objectifies Himself in his Image and unites Himself
therewith in the Love that is Himself. Refuting the social
doctrine of the Trinity, Aquinas says that God needs no
fellow (*consociatus*), since he has all good in 'One Person'
(1, 32, 1 ad. 2). It is a prophetic statement, in which though
it is not exactly in his mind, Aquinas virtually reaches
the doctrine of the One Personal God, in whom the
'Persons' of the Athanasian Creed are τρόποι ὑπάρξεως.
Seinsweisen, Modes of Being, 'moments' in the Divine life.
Indeed that is what his whole doctrine points to. All that
is necessary to transform virtuality into actuality is the
notion of self-consciousness which modern philosophy
owes to the genius of Fichte. It is the nature of the self,
first to objectify itself, and then to find satisfaction in
the objectification. With finite and imperfect selves this
is a process; with God the Absolute and Perfect Personality
it is a *totum simul*. God completely and eternally objectifies Himself and is satisfied. He can have no higher
or worthier object of love than Himself. He is at once
Love and the source of all love.

We have now arrived at the conclusion to be drawn
from our historical study. It can be stated in a sentence:
the Christology of Schleiermacher must be combined with
the Trinitarianism of Aquinas as reinterpreted by Barth.
To work out all the consequences of this position would
require another book and that a long one. But to make it
secure there is one thing that even now must be attempted.
It is to show how Phil. ii. 5–11 is to be interpreted in the
light of it. Does it still allow us to say, 'Love came down
at Christmas'? Here is an essential test of its truth.

It must be admitted that the social doctrine of the Trinity seems here to have an advantage. Even when a timeless truth is substituted for an impossible bit of history, there still remains a sufficient distinction of the Persons, to justify the popular view that the Son of God 'descended from heaven'. Thus there is a closer approximation to creed, hymn and liturgy.

The solution of the difficulty may be in two stages, firstly, a discussion of the particular point before us, and secondly, a reflection on the general principle involved. As to the first point, there is help in some most remarkable words of Augustine (*Ench.*, 36). Reference was made to the passage before. The Incarnation, he says stands as a supreme example of Divine grace apart from all merit, 'that men may understand that they are justified from sin by the same grace, by which it was brought about that the man Christ could have no sin'. Here Augustine transcends the traditional Christology. Cp. Lk. ii. 40.

God chose Israel, He sent Christ, He gave the Spirit— all in grace. He communicated Himself to Israel and especially to its prophets, and in due time He communicated Himself in Absolute Potency to Jesus, born of the stock of Israel, who was first Barth's 'human potentiality' (τὸ γεννώμενον ἅγιον, Lk. i. 35), and then Origen's 'pure soul' (Lk. ii. 52). So it was that as the Divine grace filled Christ's human consciousness and completely dominated it, He remained a man like other men, and was yet the Word of God made flesh, who through the communication of His consciousness of God to others in the Spirit is the Saviour of the World. Thus it stands true that 'Love came down at Christmas', from eternity into time, once for all, and yet for always.

The general principle involved in the above argument has been stated by Anselm in his *Cur Deus Homo*. Dealing with a certain time-honoured view of the Atonement, he says that it can readily be admitted as a figurative adornment of the truth, if a solid substance of truth first be found. Anselm speaks in the language of objectivity. Schleiermacher makes the same point in the modern language of subjectivity, when he distinguishes between the poetical, rhetorical and scientific expressions of the Christian faith. Keeping the language of subjectivity, we may say that it is the arduous work of theology to find a central point of view from which the poetical and rhetorical forms of expressing the Christian faith, which as imaginative and emotional beings we can never do without, may be understood in a right perspective. To furnish such a perspective for the understanding of the doctrines of the Trinity and the Incarnation in their historical development, and to show how they may be understood to-day, is the purpose of this study.

I will end as I began with a quotation from a medieval writer. Richard of St. Victor says (*De Trinitate*, III, 1): 'What if it be not granted me to arrive at my destination? What if I fail in the race? Yet will I rejoice in seeking the face of my Lord, to have run, toiled and sweated as I have had strength.' Though I have come to a conclusion different from his, I have unity with him in endeavour.

SHORT BIBLIOGRAPHY

THIS is only a small selection from the immense literature of the subject, but the following works are mentioned as having been particularly useful besides the fundamental texts mentioned in the study.

IN GERMAN

F. C. Baur. *Die christliche Lehre von der Dreieinigkeit und Menschwerdung Gottes*, 1841–3.

R. Bultmann. *Theologie des neuen Testaments*, 1948, 1951.

E. Günther. *Die Entwicklung der Lehre von der Person Christi im neunzehnter Jahrhundert*, 1911.

A. Harnack. *Lehrbuch der Dogmengeschichte⁴*, 1906 (also in E.T.).

H. J. Holtzmann. *Lehrbuch der neutestamentlichen Theologie²*, 1911.

F. Loofs. *Leitfaden zum Studium der Dogmengeschichte⁴*, 1906; also *Paulus von Samosata*, 1924.

R. Seeberg. *Lehrbuch der Dogmengeschichte²*, 1908–17.

IN ENGLISH

D. M. Baillie. *God was in Christ*, 1948.

C. H. Dodd. *The Apostolic Preaching and Its Developments*, 1936.

A. M. Hunter. *The Unity of the New Testament*, 1942.

W. Manson. *Jesus the Messiah*, 1943.

J. K. Mozley. *Some Tendencies in British Theology*, 1951.

G. L. Prestige. *God in Patristic Thought*, 1936.

A. E. J. Rawlinson (Ed.). *Essays on the Trinity and the Incarnation*, 1928.

C. van Til. *The New Modernism*, 1946.

C. C. J. Webb. *God and Personality*, 1919.

INDEX

DATE DUE